Study
Secrets

The Backpack Study Series

Backpack Study Secrets
Backpack Speed-Reading Secrets
Backpack Term Paper Secrets
Backpack Test-Taking Secrets

Study Secrets

BACKPACK
STUDY SERIES

**Learn faster, study smarter,
and get great grades**

Steven Frank

Adams Media Corporation
HOLBROOK, MASSACHUSETTS

Published by
Adams Media Corporation
260 Center Street, Holbrook, MA 02343

ISBN: 1-58062-024-8

Printed in Canada.

J I H G F E D C B A

Library of Congress Cataloging-in-Publication Data
Frank, Steven.
Study secrets / Steven Frank.
    p.   cm. — (Backpack study series)
        ISBN 1-58062-024-8
1. Study skills — United States. I. Title. II. Series.
    LB2395.F67   1998
    371.3'1— dc21   98-6272
                        CIP

This publication is designed to provide accurate and authoritative information with regard
to the subject matter covered. It is sold with the understanding that the publisher is not
engaged in rendering legal, accounting, or other professional advice. If legal advice or
other expert assistance is required, the services of a competent professional person should
be sought.
— From a *Declaration of Principles* jointly adopted by a Committee of the American
Bar Association and a Committee of Publishers and Associations

This book is available at quantity discounts for bulk purchases.
For information, call 1-800-872-5627 (in Massachusetts, 781-767-8100).

Visit our home page at http://www.adamsmedia.com

Contents

Introduction:

Secrets of Successful Students

Study Myths

What does it take to be a successful student? If you don't know any better, you might believe these myths:

The Genius

When he was two years old, the Genius was given an IQ test and his score topped the charts. By the age of ten, he was proving complex geometric theorems and conversing in Latin. When he goes to college (only as a formality — he needs a diploma to get a job), the work is a cinch. With his photographic memory and total recall, he never needs to take notes during lectures; it all comes back to him instantly, without any effort. He also never has trouble understanding anything, so he never has to ask for help. During exams, he laughs to himself at how easy the questions are, and he is always the first person to finish. Of course, he receives straight A's.

> Success in school does not depend on being naturally gifted or a workaholic. It's more a matter of developing effective study habits.

The Workaholic

The Workaholic reads everything assigned by the professor not once or twice, but five times. She attends each and every class, even if she is so sick she can barely move, and she writes down every word the professor says. At home, she rewrites the notes meticulously, in different colors in three separate notebooks. She spends her "free" time in the library, reading her notes over and over again. She takes the entire semester to research and write an essay, and her professors are always impressed by the enormous number of sources she includes in her bibliography. Before exams, she refuses to eat or sleep so she can spend twenty-four hours a day studying. She is happy to find that she does receive As in her courses — even if she didn't have time to go to movies, make friends, or participate in extracurricular activities.

To hear these stories, you'd think that high grades only go to the supersmart or the superhuman workers. Sure, some people are naturally gifted and don't have to work all that hard, but they make up only a small percentage of the population. Others manage to get good grades without the benefit of an astoundingly high IQ, and they don't necessarily spend every minute of every day poring over the books, sacrificing their social lives and personal happiness. So, if it's not a question of innate intelligence or being willing to work day and night, what is the secret of school success?

The answer is having the right study skills. Regardless of what you study, the *way* you study can make the difference between an A and an F. And the good news is that these skills can be learned. Just as people aren't born knowing how to hit a baseball or play the piano, you can *develop* the skills that will enable you to learn new material and truly understand it.

No one is born knowing how to study. Unfortunately, there isn't nearly as much opportunity to learn how to study as there is to play baseball or the piano. Everyone assumes students will somehow figure out how they are supposed to study. Some, through trial and error, are able to develop the skills that make them successful; others need more guidance.

Study Secrets addresses all the basic skills that comprise studying — work you do in and outside the classroom, from before the start of the semester through finals — and outlines methods and techniques that will help you to become a much more efficient and successful student. These strategies can be used by anyone who wants to improve their study skills and try to raise their grades. It can be particularly helpful for students in their first years of college, when the stakes are raised and you have to study much more than you ever have before. Unless you develop study skills pretty quickly then, you're in for a rough time. However, the skills in this book can also be used by high school students who want to improve their performance for their current classes while gaining skills to prepare them for the college-level work that awaits them.

One of the study strategies discussed in this book is learning how to identify major themes of different subjects you study and then connect specific topics and ideas to those larger themes. In doing so, you gain a more comprehensive education; rather than memorizing a bunch of seemingly random and meaningless details, you work to connect ideas together. That way, you actually come to understand something and make it a part of your overall knowledge. And that means you might be able to apply those ideas to other areas. You'll see later in this book how tracking larger themes can help you take better notes in the classroom and then study from those notes for an exam.

In this introduction, we're going to start by identifying some of the major concepts and themes underlying *all* of the strategies described here for being a more successful student.

Setting Goals

One of the major techniques discussed in this book is keeping the big picture in mind as you study. It's all too easy to become so caught up in the details and requirements of specific assignments and tasks that you lose sight of what you are studying and why. Without a sense of this big picture, you can easily feel unfocused; however, if you

> Always keep in mind the "big" picture. Set specific and long-term goals, and keep them in mind as you go about your studies.

maintain a clear sense of what you are doing and why, you are more likely to remain on track.

It is also important to maintain a sense of the big picture throughout your education. You can become so involved in the intricacies of specific classes, assignments, and requirements that you forget what you're doing it all for in the first place.

Your "big picture" is a personal one, and it can be different from everyone else's. The important thing is that you remain aware of what your big picture is. Throughout your studies, as you become immersed in the details of various subjects and tasks, make certain that you step back every so often to appreciate that big picture. Try to see how each task you go about fits into it. If you see how each task contributes something of use to you personally, you'll remain much more focused on your work; you'll also find your studies more fulfilling.

You can maintain sight of the big picture by setting goals for yourself. For each task, you should set a short-term goal, such as reading a chapter of a textbook thoroughly or studying for an upcoming exam. At the same time, though, you should set larger goals — for the week, the term, the year, and even for your entire education —

and understand how all of the short-term goals help you get closer to the big ones.

To determine your overall, personal "big picture," consider your purpose in attending school. If the only reason is because your parents said you must, you are not going to be very happy. There must be something you hope to gain in your studies, and it doesn't necessarily have to be the same thing your parents or teachers want. You may, for example, want to develop specific skills to help you in a certain career. Or, you might want to receive high grades so you can get into the graduate school of your choice. There might be more personal factors involved as well, such as the desire to better yourself, to become a more educated person, and to experience new ways of thinking and seeing.

Passive vs. Active Studying

Although they don't realize it, many students approach studying as a *passive* activity. They think that as long as they look at their notes and read their textbooks they are covering the material adequately. This approach to studying is not much different from watching television: You simply look, listen, and somehow "take it all in." But you probably are never going to have an exam on a particular television show.

Try to be an active rather than passive student; the more actively involved you are with your studies, the more you'll learn, understand, and retain.

The material you study in school, though, is different; you *will* be tested on it, and you need to recall information in great detail. Moreover, you will often need to take information you've learned and apply it to other areas. Sitting back and "taking it all in" is therefore not going to cut it.

Rather than approaching studying in this passive manner, this book repeatedly emphasizes that the secret to study success is studying actively. *Active* studying means you *do* something. Instead of merely looking at and listening to new material, you *think* about it and, in the process, make it a part of your general knowledge. As a result, you are better able to remember the information for exams and also to apply it to other situations.

You'll find that all the strategies in this book include methods to involve you actively in your studies. In a general sense, though, you need to establish yourself as an active student right from the start. That means acknowledging that your education involves work — hard work. Even though you might be sitting at a desk or lying on the couch reading over notes, your mind must remain hard at work. As soon as you slip into a passive mode, the material before you will be lost, and you might as well have been watching television.

Communication Is the Key

When people think about education, they tend to view it as centering on teaching and learning. However, for both students and teachers, the essence of school is communication. Information is communicated to you by teachers and through textbooks. You, in turn, are expected to communicate back to professors (and sometimes peers) your understanding of the material through exams, papers, and presentations.

If you've ever traveled to a foreign country, you know how difficult it can be to communicate with someone who speaks a different language. While it poses a challenge, the language barrier is also one of the things that makes traveling so exciting, as you work to understand things and, in turn, to make yourself understood. Communication in school can also be very difficult. The language is somewhat different from the language you are used to speaking. Professors speak differently from your friends, and textbooks and other academic resources are written in a unique style. Not only the new vocabulary of the new information but also the way it is presented will seem strange.

In this book, you'll learn how to become a better student by becoming better at communication in the academic world. A key to success in school is learning how to translate the information being communicated to you — in classroom lectures and textbooks — into a language you understand. On exams and in papers, you then communicate back to your teachers everything you've learned.

> Mastering communication skills is a key to being a successful student — the information communicated to you in books and from teachers, the information you communicate back on exams and papers, and everything you communicate to yourself in the process.

Of course, in studying, what you are primarily concerned with is how you communicate to yourself. While teachers and books might impart facts, theories, and various kinds of information, it will all be meaningless unless you understand for yourself what you are learning. Studying, as you'll see, is a matter of engaging in a constant dialogue with yourself, during which you ask yourself questions, attempt to answer them, and then ask more questions.

You should feel good knowing that you can learn how to communicate better, just as you can learn to play baseball or the piano better. That means you can learn how to be a more efficient, more successful student. And you don't need to be a genius or a workaholic to do it.

Getting — and Staying — Organized

Being a student is the equivalent of having a full-time job and then some. You have a tremendous number and range of responsibilities — and making it even more stressful, those responsibilities will change week by week, course by course, semester by semester. If you don't keep a clear head

Try to become organized. Keep a clear head and approach tasks in a logical, step-by-step fashion. Keep track of appointments and responsibilities, and keep your work and study spaces neat.

and keep track of everything you need to do, you're certain to forget some vital task. And if you don't have a logical approach to these tasks, you'll work inefficiently, wasting time and winding up with less than satisfactory results. This book provides step-by-step, logical approaches to most study tasks and responsibilities, as well as other organizational tips. However, in addition to following these overall techniques, you must work at being a more organized individual in general. Some people are more organized by nature, but anyone can learn how to be more organized. In general, try to keep a clear head at all times, plan every task well ahead, and go about your work in logical, step-by-step stages. Keep track of all your responsibilities and appointments, and keep your study space neat so you can always find things you need. You'll read more about getting organized later on.

Making It a Habit

There's more to being a student than individual duties like reading textbooks and taking notes in the classroom. In addition to learning the best way to approach these study tasks, you've got to adopt an effective overall study routine for everything you do. In this book, you'll read about the various habits you should make part of your study routine.

As a student, you are faced with so many tasks and responsibilities, it can seem overwhelming. The key to making it all manageable is making it all a matter of habit. The more routine something is, the less effort it requires. Think about your morning routine. You probably go through the same ritual every day — showering, brushing your teeth, taking vitamins — without thinking about it. If you also make study tasks a habit, they'll come as easily as brushing your teeth.

However, you must adopt the right habits. After all, not all habits are necessarily good. Once a habit is set, it becomes hard to break. By making the strategies and approaches outlined in this book a part of your general study routine, you guarantee you will adopt the right habits for school success.

Preparations

As we noted in the introduction, it's crucial that you be organized as you approach your work. But being an organized student doesn't begin when you enter the classroom. A key to being organized throughout the school year is making advance preparations *before* school even starts. This chapter describes several things you can do before the first day of class that will make everything easier for you during the year — and put you well on the way to study success.

Choosing a School

The kind of experience you have as a student — including your academic success — will depend to a large extent on the school you go to. When it comes to high school, you probably do not have much choice in which school you attend (unless you are applying to private schools). However, if you are planning on attending college, you will likely have a role in making the decision. Make certain you give the decision careful thought. There are thousands of colleges and universities out there, but only a handful are going to suit your interests and needs. If you are generally unhappy at your school, you're going to find it difficult to work efficiently. Don't choose a school haphazardly based on what other people tell you or where you think you should go.

Researching Schools

Do some research. There are many different sources of information you can consult. Because the following sources do not all provide the same kind of information, you should consult several of them. The more information you have, the more well-rounded the picture of the school you're researching will be:

College Guides. There are almost as many college guides on the market as there are colleges. Many guides simply list basic facts about the schools, such as the number of students, the student/teacher ratio, requirements to graduate, majors offered, and average SAT scores of those admitted; other more subjective guides try to paint a portrait of life at the school and elaborate on each school's strengths and weaknesses. Both kinds of books can be quite valuable, particularly in the early stages of your college search when you are identifying schools that are right for you. As you narrow down your choices, you can get more detailed information from other sources. Look carefully at recent statistics about the school. How many people drop out before graduating? How long does it take most students to get a degree? What percentage go on to find jobs within a year of graduating?

What percentage go on to graduate or professional schools? If these statistics are poor, the school may not provide its students with everything it should.

Web Sites. Many colleges and universities now have their own Web sites on the Internet. If you have access, you can visit these sites and get a variety of information about a school. Check the World Wide Web yellow pages for listings. There are also several on-line college guides, many provided by the same publishers as the college guide books you see in the bookstore.

Information Directly from Colleges. You can write to specific schools and request information. Keep in mind that their brochures are designed to present the school in the best possible light. Still, the brochure will provide important basic information. Additionally, try to get the course catalog so you can get an idea of the course offerings.

Friends and Relatives. Ask people where they went to school (or are currently going) and how they feel about it. Ask specific questions about assets and drawbacks. Keep in mind, though, that people are different. What one person may have loved or hated about the school may not affect you the same way. Be wary especially of the "Legacy Trap" — just because a close relative went to a particular school and loved it does not mean it's necessarily the best place for you. Consider your own interests and needs, and find a school that meets them.

Campus Visits. Visiting a school is an excellent way to get a tremendous amount of information about it. You'll see the campus the way it really looks, not as it appears in the glossy brochure photos. Go on a campus tour and check out the admissions office, where there is often some kind of information session for prospective students. Make certain you talk to students; they will give you an accurate assessment of the school from the student's point of view. If possible, arrange to stay overnight in a dormitory (most schools make this experience available to applicants). Of course, visiting schools is time-consuming and can be expensive; you should plan to visit only those schools you are seriously considering attending.

Factors to Consider in Making the Big Decision

As you attempt to narrow down your list of possible choices, there are several important factors that you should keep in mind:

Size. Schools range in size from student populations of a few hundred to several thousand. The size of the student body can affect your experiences in particular ways. A smaller school has the advantage of making it easier to meet and get to know people, including your fellow students, teachers, and administrators. At the same time, a smaller school may have limited academic and social offerings. A larger school will likely have more to offer — there will always be more people to meet and socialize with — but it might also be easier to feel lost or isolated, as seeking out people and resources will be more of a challenge.

4

> Choose your school carefully. Conduct research and consider various factors that are important to you as you make your decision.

At the same time, the size of the student population won't necessarily be an indication of the amount and kinds of academic offerings and resources, nor of the student/teacher ratio. Don't necessarily eliminate a school from consideration solely based on the population without looking more carefully at other factors.

Academic Offerings and Resources. If you have decided on a program of study or major, you will then want to look particularly at those schools offering courses and programs in that area. Depending on the area in which you are interested, you might also want to consider the kinds of resources (such as laboratories, specialty libraries, expert faculty) the school has that cater to that subject area. Even if you have not yet decided on a particular major (as is the case with many students), you probably have a general idea of which subjects interest you. You would therefore want to make certain that classes in those subjects are available at the school of your choice. In addition to fields that already interest you, look at other departments and fields to see what else is offered. If you are uncertain of a major, or in case you change your mind, you might like to know there are other possibilities.

Social Life/Student Population. Your entire college experience will not be spent in a classroom, naturally. You might want to consider then what options are available for you in addition to academics. Find out what kinds of extracurricular activities and organizations are at the schools you're considering and see if there is anything that interests you. You might also investigate what students do during their free time and try to determine if you would find activities that interest you. Are there organized campus social activities, such as concerts or visiting performers? Are students into partying or campus sports? If you go visit a school and/or talk to students there, you can ask what social activities students tend to enjoy in addition to the social and extracurricular activities offered by the school.

You also may want to consider the profile of the student population in terms of factors such as gender, ethnicity, class, religion, and sexuality. Is it important to you to be with students who are similar to yourself? Do you want to go to a school with a diverse student population? You can think about these issues in advance and consider them as you look at schools.

Location. Do you want to go to a city school, suburban school, or rural school? Do you prefer a change of seasons, or sunny weather all year? To some people, where they attend school plays a big part in how comfortable they feel. City schools have the advantage of having lots of activities and excitement readily available, but they generally won't have a central campus and you'll have to grapple with big city problems such as noise and pollution. Rural campuses will often be breathtakingly beautiful, but they can be in isolated locations. A campus visit will really help you determine if a school's atmosphere is right for you. Keep in mind that it can take some time to adjust to a new location, especially if you choose a school in an environment different from that to which you are accustomed.

Finances. A major factor in determining which school you attend will likely be the tuition and living expenses, and how much you can afford. As you begin considering schools, you should talk with your parents or some other advisor about your financial situation. How much of your education can be paid for by family members? How much are you going to be responsible for yourself? If your budget is somewhat limited, you don't necessarily have to eliminate certain schools from your list. Instead, you should begin to investigate the many forms of financial aid that are available. Most schools offer some kind of financial aid that you might apply for, including various scholarships and work-study opportunities. You can also consider taking out a loan and investigate different kinds of national scholarships that are available. The guidance office at your high school should be able to provide information about this for you.

Whatever school you choose, it will likely take a period of adjustment for you to begin to feel comfortable. However, if by the end of the first year, you find the school is not what you had hoped it would be, or that you are unhappy, you can consider transferring.

> Find out about all course requirements—general requirements for graduation and specific requirements for your major or concentration.

Choosing Courses

Consider the Requirements

Before a semester starts, you'll have to pick your courses. If you're in high school, many of your courses will be predetermined, but you might still have some choices. In college, you'll have to choose all of your classes. Either way, it's imperative that you find out what the requirements are for you to graduate. For both high school and college, there will be set requirements of the number and kinds of classes you need to take to graduate. Make certain you find out well in advance what those are so that you can plan your schedule accordingly. It would be a real problem to find out a few days before graduation that you never took a particular course required to get your degree.

At most colleges, there will be certain general requirements for all students. There might be several general fields of study (such as arts and literature, history and social science, math and science, etc.), and you can have some choice in determining which courses you take within each field. There might also be requirements, e.g., special freshman seminars, writing workshops, and physical education.

Once you determine a major, there will then be special requirements for that field.

Get as much information as you can about requirements as early as possible. Most of this information will be included in the course catalog from the school; read those sections over carefully. There also might be printed information available from administration or department offices. For specific requirements for a certain major, your best bet is probably to go to that department and ask if they have information they can give you. It can be tricky deciphering all the requirements; you should feel free to seek out help. Talk to your advisor in planning your schedule and ask specifically about the requirements. There also might be an academic advising center or guidance center where you can speak to someone and ask questions.

Many courses will have prerequisites. These are other courses you must have already taken before you may take a particular course. Make certain when deciding on courses that you check to see whether there are prerequisites. If there are prerequisites and you have not already taken them, DO NOT register for the course. Instead, you might consider taking one of the prerequisite courses so that later on you will be fully prepared for the particular course in which you were originally interested.

Make Informed Choices
Although you'll have to fulfill certain requirements, you'll still have to make choices in figuring out your schedule. Most schools have a tremendous variety of offerings;

there are many different courses as well as many different teachers. However, both teachers and courses can range in quality. It would really be a shame to spend money for college credits and wind up in courses in which you just don't learn anything.

Before you select classes, do some research. Think about whether the subject matter is interesting to you. Read the course description in the catalog and find out if there is a sample syllabus available to look at — ask at the department office. Try to talk to other students who have already taken this course. Ask them what their experiences were like and whether they would recommend the course. Get them to talk as specifically as possible about what topics were covered. You can also check out the reading list to see if it looks interesting. You can go to the bookstore to look over the books themselves.

More often than not, the deciding factor in what you get out of a particular course is the professor. A dynamic teacher can make the most mundane of subjects seem interesting. However, a poor teacher can make the most fascinating subject matter a total bore.

To find out about a particular professor, ask around and talk to fellow students. Don't assume that just because a professor is famous or has won awards that he is a good teacher; schools often hire big-name professors for their academic reputations, not for their teaching abilities. If you are thinking of taking a certain course, ask friends if they've ever had that particular professor and what they thought of him. You might even try sitting in on a professor's class to

Choose courses carefully. Conduct research and find out about the course and professor before you choose.

see what he is like. Many schools also make available course evaluations written by students who took the class previously. These evaluations might be available as a publication, or on file in the department. Ask in the department if there are any evaluations and where you might find them.

If you are in high school, you probably don't have as much choice in determining what courses and teachers you have. However, you do have some opportunities to make decisions about what you study. For example, you'll usually have to choose a few elective courses each year. Whenever you do have some choice, be an educated consumer. Do some research about the course and the teacher before you sign up for anything.

Tools of the Trade: Buying Supplies

Throughout the semester, you're going to need a variety of supplies and materials for your classes and schoolwork. The more you can track down and purchase early on, the less you'll have to worry about later when you are immersed in classes, schoolwork, and studying. Certain basic supplies, such as pens and paper, you'll need for all of your classes each term; these you can certainly buy well in advance. In addition to the basic supplies you'll need for all of your classes, there will be special books and materials you'll need for each class. Make certain you find out what these are and purchase them as early as possible in the semester. These materials will likely be listed on the course syllabus if your teacher gives you one. If not, you can feel free to ask the professor during the first week what supplies you might need.

The Basics: Pen and Paper

The most important tools you'll need as a student are paper and writing utensils for taking notes in class. When you go to the stationery shop or bookstore, you'll see hundreds of types of supplies, from legal pads to spiral notebooks to high-tech notebook "systems" that promise to do everything from keeping a time schedule to programming a VCR.

The best way to keep notes, though, is on loose-leaf paper (that's the kind with three holes that you can put in and take out of a notebook). There are several reasons why this is recommended. For one thing, you won't have to lug your entire notebook to class. You can simply keep some loose-leaf paper in a folder or small binder that you carry throughout the day to all your classes. When you get home, you can then transfer the relevant sheets into your permanent binder(s). You can either keep separate binders for different subjects or one big binder with different subjects separated by dividers.

By not carrying all your notebooks with you, you not only save your back muscles, but you also buy yourself insurance. There's always the danger that you'll lose or misplace a notebook at some point, and, if you're really unlucky, it will happen late in the semester when it will be tough to make up the lost material. If you lose a folder containing just that day's notes, it's not so traumatic.

Loose-leaf paper also enables you to move sheets around in the binders. You can add additional notes, rewrite notes, or shift things around without much difficulty. As you'll see, this flexibility will help you take notes that are more accurate and that better prepare you for exams.

You do not necessarily have to use loose-leaf paper and binders for taking notes. Some students prefer to take notes on legal pads or in spiral notebooks. If you prefer to do this, it is best to have a separate notebook for each class. Again, this will make it somewhat easier as you only need to carry around books for that day's classes; you also minimize the risk of losing all of your notes at once.

It's a good idea to have paper on hand for purposes other than taking notes in class. You might, for example, need extra paper when you conduct research for a paper or work on a special assignment or project. You can buy some extra notepads or notebooks and keep them aside for use throughout the term.

In terms of what to write with when taking notes, you should select a decent ballpoint pen. Pencils may seem like a good idea because you can erase and change things with them; however, pencils break and wear down, leaving you to sharpen them in the midst of class. Pencil is also harder to read than ink, so write with a pen! You can always cross something out if you make a mistake. Just avoid those inky, fine-point pens that leave smudges all over the paper, not to mention your hands. Pens also have a way of running out at inconvenient times (like in the middle of a lecture or exam), so buy several pens at the start of the term, and always bring an extra with you to class.

Even though it is not recommended you take notes with pencil, you might need to use pencils for certain courses, such as those in which you have to work out mathematical problems. It's worth it to buy a bunch of pencils and a good sharpener in advance and also have those on hand. You can buy a small hand-held sharpener that you can carry with you to class. You might, though, want an electric or battery operated one at home as they work much better.

Some students like to take notes with several colored pens or highlighters. For example, they might put key terms and phrases in one color, and the definitions of those terms in another. Doing this helps some people retain information more effectively when they study. However, taking notes in different colors is time-consuming, and therefore not necessarily recommended. While attending class, you should remain focused on the teacher, not on color-coding your notes. If you would like to color-code your notes, wait until you are out of class and have more time. But don't feel you have to color-code your notes in order to study efficiently; as you'll see, the strategies outlined in this book provide you with a number of ways of retaining information, without having to spend time juggling your pens.

Textbooks and Other Readings

For most classes you will have required readings throughout the term. These readings might be in textbooks, trade books, or special course packets compiled by the professor. You should find out what the required readings are during the first week of classes and track down as many as possible. The readings should be listed on the course syllabus. If they are not, you can ask the professor if there are any books you need to get for the course.

If you can afford it, it's a good idea to purchase required books and study materials (like course reading packets); that way, you'll have them readily available and can make any notes you like in them. If your college has its own bookstore, the books should be available there. When you go to the store, make certain you have the course numbers with you. Find the course on the shelf (you can ask a clerk for help). Make certain the books you are purchasing are the same as those listed on your schedule. Sometimes the store can make a mistake and order the wrong titles.

If you know in advance what courses you are taking, you might want to go to the bookstore before classes start and buy some of the books. That way you can avoid the crowds that will be there at the start of the semester. The slight risk in doing this is that the teacher may have changed the required readings. If you purchase a book that is not being used for your course, see if the bookstore will let you return it.

If you cannot afford to buy all of the books you need, you have several options. You can buy many books used, either at your college bookstore or at local used bookstores.

Purchase supplies and books as early as possible. Make certain you find out what books and supplies are needed during the first week of classes.

If you are going to buy used books, take the time to flip through whatever copies are there and try to find one that is not marked up much. If the book does have markings and notes, try your best to ignore them when you do the reading. It's important that you have a fresh approach to the reading and only take notes on what is relevant to you.

You may be able to check out many of the books from either your school library or a local public library. This is risky in that the library may not own the book, or the book might have been taken out by another student. You'll also have to be careful to go to the library throughout the semester to look for books well in advance of the day the reading is to be discussed in class. Some of the readings may be put on reserve by the professor (again, you can ask about this during the first week), which means they will remain in the library throughout the term. If the book or article is on reserve, you'll have to read it while remaining in the library, or you can make a photocopy. When you go to the library, you might find that another student has the reserved reading, and you'll have to come back when it is available. Again, leave yourself plenty of time to do reserved readings, well in advance of the due date.

You might consider buying some books, and taking out others from the library. If your professor passes out a schedule of readings or syllabus for the semester, you can consult it to see if there are particular sources that are used more than others. You can also ask the professor if any of the books are especially important. You can then purchase those books that are used more frequently, and go the library for the others.

It also doesn't hurt to ask friends and colleagues if they have books you could borrow or purchase from them. Many college courses are offered repeatedly, and there's a good chance someone you know already owns the book you're looking for. Some students also try sharing books with friends who are taking the same classes. This is a tricky situation, but it can work if you have a good relationship with your friend and can work out a fair schedule that allows each of you enough time to do the reading. Just remember, you'll both probably want to consult the books around exam time and will need to work a bit harder to accommodate each other's schedules.

Many college bookstores allow you to sell your books back at the end of the term. If you can afford to keep your books, you should do so. You never know when you might need a particular book again. However, if money is tight, sell as many books as you can (either to the bookstore or to anyone who is interested in buying any of your books). Try to save that money to purchase books for the next term.

Reference Books All Students Should Own
In addition to the books you'll need to get for specific courses, there are certain reference guides that are worth

purchasing and holding onto, as they can help you throughout your education. These books will prove themselves indispensable as you study, from helping you to write essays and papers to enabling you to look up additional information as you read required texts and your classroom notes. As with books for classes, reference books range in price depending on whether they are new or used, hardcover or paperback, or older or more recent editions.

Collegiate Dictionary.   This is the most important reference book for a student to own. As you go about your required reading for courses, you'll encounter many new vocabulary words you'll need to know in order to understand what you read. Additionally, as you write essays, you should double-check the spelling and meaning of any words for which you are not 100 percent certain of the correct usage.

Thesaurus (preferably in dictionary format).   This is a resource for improving your writing. By looking up synonyms for frequently used words, you can alter your usage and make your writing much more interesting.

Specialized Dictionary.   There are many of these dictionaries on the market that list words, names, and terms within specific fields, such as literature, science, philosophy, and mythology. Depending on what areas you study, you may wish to purchase one or more of these guides.

World Atlas. You'd be surprised how much information you can get from a good atlas. As you read or write, you can dip into it for various facts, from identifying capitals to basic information about countries. As you come across a place name in your reading, you can enhance your sense of it and of its place in the world by opening your atlas.

Grammar Handbook. Turning in essays that are grammatically correct is extremely important; using proper grammar tells your teacher that you are a serious student who takes pride in your work. There are, of course, so many different rules and exceptions to the rules that it is difficult to know them all by heart. If you own a good grammar handbook, you can dip into it and double-check any rules that give you trouble.

Style and/or Essay Format Manual. In addition to writing with proper grammar, it is also important that you are consistent in your style and format. Be consistent first and foremost with how you cite outside sources and list them in your bibliography. Depending on which format your teacher instructs you to follow, make certain you purchase a format guide, such as the MLA or APA handbook. Also, be consistent throughout your writing with punctuation and language usage. A style book such as *The New York Times Manual of Style and Usage* will help you with this.

Almanac. Owning an almanac may seem silly, but you'll be surprised how much useful information it contains. You never know when you'll need some tidbit for a paper you're writing. Dip into the almanac for looking up miscellaneous facts and figures, from past Academy Award winners to a list of the U.S. presidents and their birthplaces.

Date Book/Wall Calendar

Before you begin classes, make sure to buy a pocket date book and/or wall calendar for keeping a record of all your assignments, appointments, and responsibilities. This will help you stay organized throughout the semester, and ensure that you don't forget or miss an important deadline or date. As soon as you get the information, write down in your book assignment due dates, exam dates, appointments with professors or study partners, and extracurricular activity meetings, as well as any other obligations. Get in the habit of carrying your date book around with you so you can make additions or changes at any time. For example, you might arrive at class one day and find out that the professor has decided to change the date of the midterm exam. You can put the new date right in your calendar. That way you're certain not to forget it.

If you can afford it, you might consider purchasing an electronic pocket date book/organizer. There are currently several on the market, including some that can actually read your handwriting when you enter new information. These organizers, in addition to being capable of being reprogrammed and reused term by term, can hold tremendous amounts of information (like names and phone numbers) and often have special, helpful features (like built in alarm clocks to alert you to special appointments).

In addition to having a pocket calendar, you might also consider purchasing a wall calendar to keep at home by your desk. You can put major dates up on the calendar, like the start of classes, exam dates, and due dates for assignments. That way you'll have the advantage of seeing how tight each month is as you make plans and organize your study schedule.

A Computer

A large portion of the work you do for classes — such as essays, term papers, problem sets, lab reports, special projects — will need to be typed up and typed neatly. It is therefore pretty important that you purchase a computer. Buying your own computer is well worth the investment as it enables you to do so much. Writing essays on a computer enables you to revise, rewrite, edit, and check spelling with ease, and then print out a flawless, neat final version. You can also keep all of your essays on disk and have them readily available if you need them. There are, of course, many other uses for a computer that you might also take advantage of, from desktop publishing to keeping track of your personal finances.

Of course, buying a computer can be expensive, but it is well worth the investment, especially if you will need to write many papers. When buying a computer, consider what your priorities are. What do you plan to use the computer for most? Will the model you are looking at provide you with everything you require? Is it important to you to be able to carry the computer around from place to place? Is it important to you that the computer have enough memory to run many different programs? Do you want to have a CD-ROM? A color monitor? It might help to do some research before buying a computer. Read some computer magazines to see which models are particularly recommended for certain tasks. Ask around and find out what computers other students are using and if they would recommend them. If you know someone who is a computer expert, get him or her to go shopping with you.

If you do have limited finances, don't despair. Computers also range significantly in price. Depending on the options you choose, you may be able to find a computer that meets your needs in your price range. You might also consider buying a used computer. Again, ask around and see if someone you know is interested in selling his or her computer, or place a classified ad in the school newspaper.

Many schools also offer students special discounts if they purchase computer equipment from the school. Ask at your school bookstore, if there is one, what kind of discount you might get.

If you do not want to buy a computer, you can probably still work on one. Most schools now have computer labs in which students can work on a computer for free. You might have to sign up for time or wait for a free computer, so make certain you plan ahead and give yourself enough time to work on the essay. Many schools also offer classes and seminars on different computer programs so that you can learn how to use them. If you don't know how to use a computer, this is the time to learn and get in the habit of using it for writing essays.

Another option is to purchase an electronic typewriter. There are several sophisticated electronic typewriters on the market that function much like word processors in enabling you to make changes and revisions, and even check spelling. These typewriters will enable you to neatly type up essays and assignments, and are usually less expensive than computers. However, keep in mind that these typewriters have much more limited uses than a computer. Even if you buy an inexpensive, basic or used computer, you can always upgrade it or buy additional equipment to suit your future needs.

Either way, make sure you purchase plenty of printer or typing paper, as well as ribbons or ink jets, early on. There's nothing worse than trying to type up or print out a final version of an essay and running out of paper! Don't put yourself in that stressful situation and make certain you're fully prepared.

Other Supplies

In addition to pens, paper, and required books, there might be special materials you need for certain courses, such as lab equipment, calculators, software, or art supplies. On the first day of class, make certain you find out exactly what those materials are. Most likely, they will be listed on whatever syllabus or schedule the professor hands out. If they are not, you might want to ask the professor after class if there are any special supplies or materials you'll need.

TOOLS OF THE TRADE: A STUDENT'S SHOPPING LIST

The following items are essential for any student. Make certain you have them at the start of the school year.

____ Required textbooks and course materials (such as course packets)

____ Loose-leaf paper and binders and/or notebooks, notepads.

____ Folders with pockets (for collecting handouts in class)

____ Pens (blue or black ink)

____ Pencils, eraser, and pencil sharpener

____ A typewriter or computer (if you don't want to purchase one, make certain you have access to one)

____ Typing or printer paper

____ Stationery and envelopes

____ Diskettes (for computer use)

____ A date book or schedule/assignment book

____ A wall calendar

____ Reference guides (such as a dictionary and thesaurus)

____ A backpack, bookbag, or briefcase

____ Correction fluid (for correcting mistakes when proofreading)

____ A stapler and staples

____ Paper clips

____ Index cards (3" x 5")

____ A portable tape recorder

____ An alarm clock and wristwatch

____ Specialty items: Depending on the courses you take, you might also need a compass, calculator, graph paper, lab report sheets, slide rule, protractor, scissors, paste, markers, highlighters, and so on

These kinds of supplies will probably be available in the school bookstore or at a well-stocked stationery store. However, you might have to hunt around for specialty items or even have to place special orders by mail. That's why it's best if you shop for everything early on to give yourself plenty of time to track down your supplies long before you actually need them.

The First Week of Classes: Find Out Exactly What You're in For

Surprises can often be exciting but not when it comes to school. The last thing you want is to show up one day for class and find an unexpected exam waiting on your desk, or to find on the last day of class that you were supposed to have collected data all term for some lab assignment. In order to be fully prepared for the semester, you need to know exactly what to expect from each class — and what the professor expects from you. That way you can gain a sense of how difficult the course might be and how much time you'll have to devote to it, and plan your schedule accordingly. These are some of the questions you should try to have answered early in the semester:

1. What specific topics will be covered? Are there any prerequisites for this course?
2. Is there a set schedule of readings and discussions? Has the teacher given it to you?
3. Are there any essays or written assignments? Special projects? Problem sets? When are these assignments due? What is the exact nature of these assignments? Do they require conducting research?

Find out as much as possible about the nature of the course and what is expected of you early in the semester. Know what you're in for and plan ahead.

4. Are there exams? When will they be given? Will they be given in class? What will the format be for the exams? Will there be surprise quizzes?
5. What percentage of the overall grade is each specific assignment or requirement?
6. What is the teacher's attendance policy?
7. Is participation in class discussion important? Is it considered a part of your grade?
8. What are the teacher's general expectations from the students?

You can get a great deal of this information from reading over whatever material the professor hands out to the class. If the professor takes the time to type up a handout, chances are it's important. Don't think that unless the professor actually tells you about particular requirements you don't need to know about them. The syllabus might have important information in it that the professor won't necessarily go over in class. Make certain you read whatever the professor gives you. You can then ask the professor about any unanswered questions (from the preceding list), or any others you might have about the class. You might want to do this privately after class so as not to take up class time. In general, try to gain as complete a picture as possible about what the course will be like and what is expected of you throughout the term.

Study Tips: In the Classroom

Your Role in the Classroom

As a student, much of your time will be spent in the classroom. There are, however, many types of classroom experiences, and your role as a student can vary somewhat depending on the type of course and the professor's teaching style.

Many classes, especially in college, are lectures. This will typically be true of the more basic, survey courses that are required for many students. In these courses, which will tend to be larger, the professor speaks directly to the class and imparts information. As a student in this kind of class, your primary responsibility is to sit, listen carefully, take notes, and occasionally ask questions. If a reading has been assigned for that day, it is wise to make sure you have done it so that you can follow and understand the lecture and/or ask questions about what confuses you.

However, for other types of classes, it is absolutely imperative that you do all required readings beforehand, as your role in the class is more active. For example, in a discussion-oriented seminar, the professor or a teaching assistant will meet with a smaller group of students to talk together about certain subject matter, sharing ideas, opinions, and questions. In these classes, it is particularly important that you come to class well prepared — having done whatever reading or assignment is expected of you that day — so that you can participate fully. Many classes combine lecture and discussion. In general, the more prepared you come, the better. Be ready to listen carefully and take notes and/or participate in a discussion.

In addition to lectures and seminars, there are many "hands-on" type courses in which you actually work on some project or assignment in class. For example, many science courses will include time in a lab in which, perhaps following a demonstration by the professor, you work on experiments and then write up reports. For any of these classes, again make certain you are fully prepared for that day's work. That means reading anything assigned for that day and coming to class with whatever materials you need to do the work.

Making an Impression

There's no way around the fact that grades are a central part of most formal educations. A large portion of a grade

> It is extremely important that you try to make a good impression, especially in class, as this is the place where you will have the most interaction with the professor.

is based on objective information, such as the number of short-answer questions you got right or wrong or the number of days you attended class. However, grading is also subjective: It is based in large part on the teacher's impression of you. While this impression can't change the number of exam responses you got right or wrong, it can influence other aspects of your final grade. For example, a final grade will often reflect a grade for class participation, which is much more difficult to measure than the number of right or wrong responses.

It is extremely important that you try to make a good impression, especially in class, as this is the place where you will have the most interaction with the professor. However, you also need to be careful how you do it. If you overdo your effort, it can seem insincere and backfire. For example, if you interrupt the lecture or class discussion simply to make some comment that demonstrates how smart you are, you will not impress the teacher. Moreover, the teacher might resent that you've interrupted class for an unrelated point in an obvious attempt to gain Brownie points.

The impression you want to convey is not necessarily how smart you are, but that you are a conscientious student who is willing to work hard to learn. There are several specific things you can do to make this impression.

Attendance

Nothing is more off-putting to a teacher than a student who consistently comes late to class, or who doesn't come at all. Coming late disrupts the entire class and, more severely, indicates to the teacher that you don't care about the class. Even in a large lecture course, where you think you might slip in unnoticed, a teacher can notice a student who arrives late. You should therefore make it a habit to get to class on time. If you have a special reason for being late, make certain you see the professor during office hours to explain the situation and apologize.

Coming late to class is a disruption; not coming at all is a major problem that can seriously affect your grade. In some smaller classes, a teacher will take attendance. If this is the case, you should obviously make certain you go as often as possible. Having perfect attendance will probably impress the teacher when it comes time to make your class participation grade.

Even if a teacher does not take attendance, it is still worth going to class as often as you can. For one thing, being there on a regular basis ensures that you are exposed to all the course material, which in itself will probably improve your grades. Moreover, if you attend class regularly, the teacher will consider you a familiar face.

Office Visits

If a teacher doesn't know you by name, however, it won't matter what image she has of you when she gives you a grade. While a teacher will usually know you by name in a small class, it is almost impossible for her to know you personally in a large lecture class. You should therefore make sure to see the professor at least once during office hours to introduce yourself. To help break the ice, try to come up with a specific question to ask about the class. During the course of your discussion, you can tell the professor a bit about yourself and your academic interests. Doing this ensures that the teacher has an impression of you as an individual, not just as another face in the crowd.

Class Participation

When class participation is part of the grade, many students make the mistake of thinking that they just need to talk a lot to get a good grade. However, there are many kinds of comments and questions, and some are much more intelligent and impressive than others.

Asking questions indicates a general interest in the class. However, students who constantly raise their hands and ask very basic questions about fairly obvious points can make a bad impression — they appear too lazy to make an effort to understand something for themselves. There is, however, a way to phrase a question that sounds more intelligent. For example, if you simply raise your hand and say, "I really don't get this. What does it all mean?" you

Try to make the best impression you can by attending class regularly, coming fully prepared, asking intelligent questions, and being conscientious about your work.

sound like you just don't want to make the effort to understand the topic. However, if you say to a professor, "I see the point about Y and Z, but I'm having trouble understanding how they relate to X," you are asking a more specific question that reflects an effort to understand something. Try to make your questions very specific to indicate you have some knowledge and a genuine interest in clarifying a point.

Another way students earn credit for class participation is by making comments during class discussions. However, many students who feel compelled to say something in class will say whatever pops into their heads. If the comment restates something that has already been said or merely points out something obvious, it won't impress the teacher; in fact, it can indicate you haven't been paying close attention. If you want to make a general comment, be sure it contributes something meaningful or makes a new point.

Not everyone is comfortable participating in class discussions or asking questions in front of large groups, and this doesn't necessarily detract from the class participation portion of a grade. If you are shy, visit the professor during office hours and discuss the course — this will demonstrate that you have an active interest in the class.

Take Pride in Your Work

Being a conscientious student means you take pride in your work; it indicates you are not just going through the motions of showing up for class, but are taking your work seriously. The quality of the work you turn in indicates how conscientious you are. For example, an essay that has been carefully proofread and neatly typed shows you've put work into it and care about how it appears. However, an essay with correction fluid and pencil smudges, spelling errors, and a coffee stain on the cover page sends the message that you really don't care all that much about the work. And the teacher will then not care all that much about reading it or the grade you get.

While there are specific things to do that show how conscientious you are, you also need to adopt a conscientious attitude. That way whatever you do, whether you are conscious of doing it to impress the teacher or not, will reflect well on you. Take pride in your work as a student, take your job seriously, and everything you do will reflect this positive attitude.

Note Taking Basics

The major task you'll have in most classes is taking notes. This is especially true of lectures, where you need to document the information the professor imparts. However, you'll often need to take notes in seminars and "hands-on" classes, as well. Having accurate and informative notes from all of your classes is extremely important, as you later rely on these notes to prepare for tests.

Many students unfortunately have no idea how to take notes efficiently. Some think they need to write down every word the professor says — an act that is physically impossible unless, perhaps, you have a bionic arm. These students often panic when they miss a line or two from the professor's lecture, and then miss more of the lecture. Other students think they don't need to take any notes at all, that it's enough to sit back and listen carefully, taking it all in. But weeks later, when the exam comes up, how much can they actually remember? In this section, we'll go through a step-by-step strategy for taking notes that will help you make certain you get down what you need to have complete, helpful notes for studying later on.

Live and in Person

An essential element of note taking is remembering that it involves communication. The professor is communicating information to you, and you want to create a document of that information that communicates to you what you need to know when it's time to study.

The point of taking notes is not just getting a copy of what the teacher has told you. If that were the case, why would there be lectures at all? Wouldn't it just be easier to read it in a book? The fact is that live communication is very powerful and very effective. For example, if you were to have a telephone conversation with someone who speaks Swahili, it would be almost impossible for you to understand what he was saying (unless, of course, you happen to speak it yourself). However, if you were to have the conversation in person, you'd probably understand something. You'd be able to read body language, watch gestures, and pay attention to facial expressions, which provide information about what is being communicated. In turn, the speaker would see from your expression what you do and do not understand and adopt other techniques to try to communicate.

By attending live lectures, you can gain a deeper understanding of the material being presented. As in a conversation with someone who speaks another language, you'll receive additional information through body language, expression, and tone of voice. Also, simply by being present and listening attentively, you'll pick up more of the material than you would by merely reading. Live performance, after all, is generally more compelling and likely to hold your interest; that's why people pay so much for concert and theater tickets.

In this section, we're going to learn a method for taking effective lecture notes. We'll learn how to take notes that capture the important points covered by the professor or class instructor. We'll also learn how to write those notes in language you can understand, which will also help you learn the material. Following this method will make it much easier for you to study for exams because you will already have done much of the tough work — listening.

Strategies for Effective Listening

1. Make the Effort

The first step to effective listening is to realize that listening takes effort. It won't happen on its own and it's not something that is going to take place naturally, just by your being there. Go into situations where it's important for you to listen determined to listen, and listen carefully. Concentrate. It may be difficult at first, but in time you'll get better.

2. Pay Attention to the Speaker

It is very difficult to listen to someone if you are not giving all your attention to that person. Ideally, you should look at the person's face the entire time she is speaking. However, in a lecture this is not always possible because you also need to look at your notes from time to time. Try, if you can, to write while keeping your eye on the professor. This may make your notes more messy than usual, but, in time, you'll get more adept at writing without looking at the page. If you can't write and look at the professor at the same time, remember to look up from your notes frequently. This will ensure that you are maintaining a direct line of communication with her.

If the professor is explaining a difficult concept, you are much better off not writing and looking only at her. This way, you can concentrate on listening and understanding. After the professor is finished, jot down a few notes or phrases to help you remember what was said.

3. Minimize Distraction

To maintain that direct line of communication between you and the speaker, it's important to minimize all outside distractions. Different things can be distracting. Perhaps a friend you sit with can't resist chatting during the lecture. Even something as tame as chewing gum or a grumbling stomach can begin to sound like a major earthquake when you are trying to pay attention to something else. Choose your seat carefully and come to class well fed and prepared to listen.

You might also decide to sit closer to the professor if it helps you concentrate better. Sitting in the first few rows is not absolutely crucial; in fact, some people feel very uncomfortable being that close to the professor. However, if you are having trouble hearing or concentrating, try sitting in the first or second row. You might be surprised at how much more of the lecture you catch.

Additionally, the way you sit can also affect your ability to pay attention. If you slouch in the chair, your eyes won't be focused on the speaker. Each time you want to look at the teacher, you will have to lift up your entire head, and the effort needed to do that can disrupt your note taking. Instead, it is much more effective to sit with your back against the chair back. Place the sheet of paper in the center of the desk and hold it in place with whichever hand you do not use to write. If you sit in this position, you should be able to watch the professor while writing; you also will be able to glance down at your notes by just moving your eyes, not your entire head.

4. Watch for Lapses

Become more attuned to the times when your mind is drifting to other subjects or your eyes are wandering out the window. When this happens, focus your attention back on the speaker immediately. Be aware that everyone is prone to lapses in attention, and that if you can recognize when your mind wanders, you will begin to correct yourself much faster and not miss as much.

5. Watch for Clues from the Speaker

Listening effectively means more than paying attention to the words of the speaker. People convey a great deal of information through the *way* they speak as well as what they say. Get in the habit of concentrating on additional signals from a speaker besides spoken words. Pay attention to the speaker's tone of voice, the volume of his speech, pauses, hand gestures, and body language — these signals can enhance your understanding of the speaker's words. Additionally, by being alert to these elements in addition to spoken words, you have more to occupy your attention, ensuring that you remain actively engaged in the lecture, conversation, or discussion.

6. Work at It

Listening, like any skill, improves as you work at it. As you practice concentrating in different situations, you'll find you get better and better at it.

Effective note taking starts with effective listening.

It Begins Before You Put Pen to Paper

Taking effective notes doesn't start when you begin writing; it begins with being an effective *listener*. We take it for granted that we all know how to listen, that listening is a natural skill requiring no work at all. The truth is, listening is a difficult task and very few people know how to do it well. Have you ever been in the midst of a conversation with someone, nodding your head in agreement, and suddenly found yourself unable to respond to a question they've just asked? While you may have heard him, you weren't listening to him.

Why is listening so difficult? One reason is that we confuse *hearing* with *listening*. Hearing is *passive*; it means sound waves have reverberated in your ear, whether or not you want them to, and there's been a noise. Listening, on the other hand, is an *active* process. It implies that you must *do* something to accomplish it. It takes action and, often, work to listen well. For example, let's say you are sitting on a crowded subway train talking with a friend. You hear the noise of the train, the chatter of passengers around you, the boom box being blasted by a teenager, and, somewhere in all that, you even hear your friend. But to understand what your friend is telling you, you need to *do* something; you need to listen to distinguish her words from all the background noise.

> Develop good listening skills now and they'll last a lifetime and continue to bring you success.

The same principle applies to classroom lectures. There may not be the same amount of noise in a lecture room as on a crowded train (although there is plenty of distracting racket, from feet shuffling to heaters blowing), but you still have to work hard to listen to the professor's words. People respect someone who listens carefully. More importantly, those who listen are certain to catch important information that others don't.

A Strategy for Effective Note Taking

The next section describes the first part of a step-by-step strategy for taking more effective notes. This strategy has two stages: The first takes place during class, the second outside the classroom, which we'll cover in the next chapter.

The strategy outlined involves beginning your notes in class and finishing them later on. This method will relieve a lot of the pressure if you think you have to get down everything during a lecture. There's another major benefit to following this strategy: The extra attention you devote outside of the classroom guarantees you understand your own notes. This means that when exam time comes around, you won't have to panic because you don't remember — or worse, don't understand — things you learned earlier in the semester.

Note Taking Stage One: In the Classroom

1. Make Preparations

It's smart to get to class a few minutes early. For one thing, you'll be able to choose your seat. More seriously, though, coming in late can distract and offend the teacher, and it's never a good idea to get the professor angry. It's also difficult to begin work if you rush to class, arriving out of breath and flustered, with your thoughts on the outside world. By coming early, you can relax and decompress for a few minutes and put yourself in the right frame of mind. If you have time, you might want to look over your notes from the previous class to help focus your attention on the day's subject matter.

When you get to class, take out a new sheet of paper. Remember, as we discussed before, the best method for taking notes in class is to use loose-leaf paper. You can leave the heavy binder at home, but make certain you have plenty of loose-leaf paper with you (you never know how many notes you'll need to take for that day). If you brought notes with you from the previous class, you should still always start each class with a fresh piece of paper. This is because lectures tend to have their own separate topics or themes. By keeping separate notes, you can better identify distinct themes.

Always put the date and subject at the top of the first sheet, so you can easily put it in the proper binder or section at home. Next, you should draw a line down the page about three inches from the left, so that you have an extra wide margin (most pieces of notebook paper already have about a one-and-a-half-inch margin). Your paper will then look like this:

During class, take notes only on the right side of the margin. Leave the left side blank — you'll be using that space when you get to stage two, working on notes at home. You should also take notes on only one side of the paper; the back side will be used later.

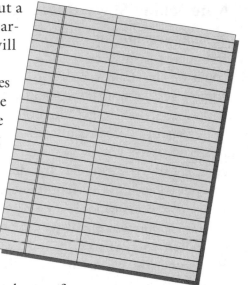

Make sure you have plenty of paper on hand throughout the lecture. Always put the date and subject on the top of each sheet; that way, if sheets from different days and classes get mixed up, you'll be able to figure out where they go. And for each new sheet, draw that line and continue taking notes only on the right side.

Leave the Tape Recorder at Home. Some students think they'll take the easy way out by bringing a tape recorder to class and relying on that instead of taking notes. However, the tape recorder ultimately means much more work than they realize. The students get home and have all that tape to sit through, which means, in effect, going to class twice.

By taking notes in class instead, you're already beginning to digest and to edit the information. For example, you might not write down information that you already know or have taken notes on previously. You also don't need to write down the detailed explanations your professor makes to recall and understand a particular concept. Since your notes are succinct, they will take far less time to read over than it would take to listen to an entire lecture on tape again.

Then there's the problem of mechanical difficulties. Tape recorders are machines. What if the batteries run out or the tape doesn't record well and you can't hear what the teacher said? What if the tape gets eaten by the machine? Minimize these risks by leaving the tape recorder at home.

There is only one way that a tape recorder may help you. If you must miss a lecture for some reason, you might want to have a friend record it so you'll be able to keep up. Make certain, though, that you listen to the lecture and take notes just as if you were sitting in class. It's also a good idea to do this before the next class so you can keep up with the course.

A Note on Laptop Computers. Some people have begun to bring laptop computers to class to take notes. While this might seem like a good idea, it's not really recommended for several reasons. For one thing, most people write by hand more quickly than they type. Also, typing on a laptop can distract your fellow students and, worse, your instructor. More importantly, writing by hand gives you greater flexibility. For example, you can jump back to previous notes to make relevant additions. You can also draw signs and use arrows and symbols more easily by hand. As you'll soon see, you'll be working a great deal with the notes you take in class, making additions and revisions. It's easier to do this on paper than on the computer.

If you want to keep your notes on your computer, you can always type them when you get home. In fact, this process is a good way to help you rethink and reorganize your notes, and it will help you remember them.

2. Write Down All Key Terms

The first and foremost commandment of note taking is this: You cannot write down everything the professor says. This is so important that it bears repeating: *You are not going to be able to write down everything the professor says!*

And what's more, if you try to write down everything the professor says, you'll find yourself in deep trouble. At some point, no matter how fast you can write, you will miss something. Either you won't hear clearly, or you'll become distracted, or your hand will cramp up. And then, if you're like many students, you'll panic. As you struggle to figure out what you missed, you'll miss even more. And before you know it, you won't have notes for the bulk of the lecture.

So let's make it clear right from the beginning. *You don't have to write down everything.* Your next question probably is, "So what exactly am I supposed to write down?" In order to answer that question, we need to examine the purpose of taking notes.

In taking notes, your aim should not be to create an exact transcript of the professor's lecture. If that were the

You don't have to write down everything the teacher says; in fact, you shouldn't even try to.

case, the professor would simply hand out photocopies. A great deal of what you hear in class might be familiar to you and, therefore, doesn't really need to be recorded. Writing down information and concepts that are new and unfamiliar should be your priority.

During lectures, the main thing professors do is communicate new information. The majority of it is often specific, such as names of people or places, significant dates, certain theories, formulas, and concepts. These are the *key terms* of the lecture.

Most often, these terms are going to be new to you, which makes them harder to remember. A goal of note taking, then, is to keep track of all these key terms.

Your professor might often write down key terms on the board. You should *always* note anything the teacher writes on the board. But there will also be many other terms that the professor might not write — if these are new to you, make certain you write them down as well.

By the way, there's a strong chance these terms will appear in the assigned reading. If you complete the reading before class, the terms will ring a bell when they come up in the lecture. Keeping up with required reading can help a great deal when you take notes, as you will feel somewhat familiar with the material. Later, we'll be talking more about the way in which reading and lectures come together and how both sources help you prepare for tests.

As you take down these key terms in class, don't worry about their correct spelling or pronunciation. Just write out words the way they sound, trying to be as accurate as you can. Later on, you can find out the right way to spell them. Believe it or not, if you write down just the key terms, you'll have a pretty accurate representation of the entire lecture. Key terms are most often the points around which the entire lecture is based. You can be certain that if you showed your professor the list of terms, she would be able to recreate the lecture for you in its entirety. Can you?

You might be surprised how much you actually remember, merely by seeing key terms. As long as you've been listening carefully, these terms can serve as triggers that help you recall much of what you heard in the lecture. Of course, you might not remember everything about each term, but chances are you can remember *something* about most of them.

Sample Lecture and Key Terms.   Following is a passage from a typical lecture, followed by a list of key terms you might include in your notes. As an exercise, try reading the lecture and creating your own list of key terms. You might even want to get a friend to read the lecture out loud while you try to list the key terms — this will come really close to the experience of being in a classroom.

> Considered by many to be the founder of modern psychoanalysis, Sigmund Freud continues to be one of the most influential, albeit controversial, figures in psychology. Living and working in turn-of-the-

century Vienna, Freud revolutionized the way in which we think of the human personality and how it is shaped and developed, not to mention the ways in which we examine our own dreams.

Among his many highly influential theories was his model of human personality. Freud conceived of personality as constructed of three distinct but conflicting entities: the *id, ego,* and *superego.* The id consists of the most basic biological drives and urges that we know from birth, including those for food, drink, physical comfort, and sexual pleasure. For this reason, Freud described the id according to the pleasure principle; that is, as the desire for instant pleasure and gratification, no matter the cost. As an infant grows, it begins to understand that the urges of the id have to be in accord with the actual circumstances of the external world. The ego then develops to satisfy the urges of the id within the workings of the real world. Rather than obey the pleasure principle, the ego adheres to the reality principle. As a child matures, it begins to internalize the morals, values, and rules set by parents and society, and in turn the superego develops. The superego is the internal judge of behavior, deeming what is good or bad, moral or immoral. It is the conscience.

Here's another way to think of the model for personality. The ego represents a person's actual, day-to-day behavior in society, the face one presents to the outside world. The id and the superego are both factors trying to influence the ego; the id pushes the ego to pursue pleasurable urges, while the superego enforces judgments, advocating "correct" behavior and warning about punishments for incorrect behavior.

According to Freud, these forces are often waged in internal, subconscious conflict that can create anxiety. One way to cure anxiety is to identify the internal conflicts that cause it.

Anxiety, Freud said, is often associated with the urges we experience as children but quickly learn are forbidden, usually when we are punished for attempting to act on them. In order to try to get rid of the anxiety, a child tries to get rid of the forbidden urge; this is known as repression, because the child pushes the thought out of its conscious deep into the subconscious, far from the face presented to the outside world. However, the forbidden urge continues to break through to the surface, sometimes throughout our lives, which can create anxiety.

To grapple with the anxiety created when the forbidden urges resurface, people create psychological defenses, which Freud called *defense mechanisms*, that protect the ego from the urges of the id. An example of a defense mechanism is *projection*, the attribution of forbidden urges to someone else (for example, instead of thinking you hate your parents, you might think your sister hates them) and *denial*, the refusal to acknowledge the urge whatsoever, even if it means completely ignoring aspects of reality (when you basically think, "No way José! Not me!"). Freud attempted to apply this theory of unconscious conflict to areas of everyday life. One example is his theory of dreams, presented in *The Interpretation of Dreams*, written in 1900. Freud said that dreams are efforts at *wish fulfillment*; they depict the gratification of the urges of the id, without the controls of the ego and superego. An example Freud often referred to was a painting called "The Prisoner's Dream," which depicts in simple terms the prisoner receiving his wish fulfillment in his dreams — his escape from jail.

However, since the forbidden urges can still create anxiety, even in dreams, they do not usually appear in such simple form; instead they are translated into images that disguise their actual meaning. Freud distinguishes between the *latent dream*, which represents the actual desires of the dreamer, and the *manifest dream*, which the dreamer actually experiences but the latent desires are presented in disguised form. Very often the manifest dream makes use of symbolism, relying on images that actually stand for something else. For example, Freud believed that dreaming of water or horses carries erotic meanings. Freud claimed that analyzing the symbols in dreams was a means of uncovering and curing the patient's anxieties.

This aspect of Freud is one of the more controversial and contested. Various studies have been conducted on patients' dreams, and they have failed to find consistent systems of dream symbols that apply to a single dreamer, let alone to many dreamers. Water and horses in my dream may mean something quite different in yours. Still, there is no ignoring how influential Freud's writings on dreams have been, not only in psychology, but also in art, music, and literature.

On a separate sheet of paper compile your own list of key terms based on the lecture above.

Here are some of the key terms for that lecture:

founder of modern psychoanalysis
Sigmund Freud
turn-of-the-century Vienna
model of human personality
id
ego
superego
pleasure principle
reality principle
subconscious conflict
anxiety
repression
defense mechanisms
projection
denial
theory of dreams
The Interpretation of Dreams (1900)
wish fulfillment
"The Prisoner's Dream"
latent dream
manifest dream

How does your list compare to the key terms included here? If you picked up on many of the same terms, then you've done a good job figuring out what is most important to write down during a classroom lecture. Now, try another simple exercise. Looking over just the list of key terms, see how much of the lecture you can remember. You'll probably find that just from this brief list you can manage to remember parts of the lecture. That should help reassure you that it's not necessary to write down every single word the professor speaks. (If you're having trouble remembering it all, don't worry. We're not done with the notes yet, and there are strategies described below to help you grasp everything important from each lecture.)

Include Brief Definitions of Key Terms. In addition to listing the key terms, you should also try whenever possible to write *brief* explanations or definitions of the terms. Again, don't write down everything the professor says. Try to jot down just a few words or phrases that will help you later on to remember what a term means.

If you can't write much about a particular term, don't worry. *Just keep listening and writing!* You'll have plenty of time to fill in more information later. If your professor has moved on to introduce a new topic or key term while you are still taking notes on a previous one, then leave that term behind.

3. Develop Your Own Shorthand

You can also develop your own kind of shorthand; this will enable you to take down more material faster and with less effort. Many study guides teach specific formulas and codes for taking notes in shorthand. The problem with these methods is that you wind up having notes that are practically written in secret code. Don't make your notes overly complicated by developing all kinds of crazy signs and formulas.

Find a way to take notes so that they make sense to you.

Here are some basic ways to develop a shorthand that is simple and easy to read. You can use any or all of these suggestions, depending on what makes the most sense to you:

Avoid Complete Sentences.   There's no reason why your notes have to be written in complete, grammatically correct sentences. Sentences are filled with words that aren't necessary for one to understand the gist of them. You can still understand the basic meaning of a sentence without using all the words in it. For example, you can leave out articles (the, a, an) and pronouns (he, she, they, it) and still understand the basic information.

The sentence:
> *You can omit the articles and pronouns from sentences and still be able to understand them.*

can be rewritten as:
> *Omit articles pronouns from sentences still understand*

Don't Worry about Spelling and Punctuation.   If you try to spell everything correctly, you'll spend too much time worrying about it. Just write things the way they

52

sound — you can check the spelling later. Sometimes using punctuation can help you write a quick definition, but it can also add unnecessary baggage to notes. You can read and understand most sentences perfectly well without it.

Keep Descriptions, Examples, and Anecdotes Brief. Very often, your professor will launch into a long description or anecdote as a means of illustrating or explaining some larger point. When the professor does this, you don't necessarily need to replicate the entire example or anecdote in your notes. You are better off listening, then using a few key words to sum up the example or anecdote. Those few words will usually be enough to trigger your memory of the entire account.

For example, a psychology professor might go into detail about various experiments and lab studies that either prove or disprove important points. You don't need to describe the whole study in your notes. You can simply write a few key words to help you remember who conducted the study, what was studied, and the result. For example, "James's Twins Study: Proved ESP doesn't work."

Abbreviate Only Repeated Key Terms. Using abbreviations is an excellent way to take notes more quickly. If you can reduce words to just a letter or two, it is obviously going to help you write faster. But be very careful. When you abbreviate too many terms, your notes become difficult to read. And if your notes don't make sense to you, then writing more quickly didn't really help you. You should therefore only abbreviate key terms that are repeated frequently throughout the lecture.

The best way to abbreviate is to use capital letters that stand for entire words. Usually you can just use the first letter of a word as its abbreviated form. It's a good idea to circle any abbreviations you use, so you'll recognize them.

The first time you come across an important term, write out the entire term and circle it. This will serve as a signal that you will be abbreviating this term from now on. Then, each time that term comes up, use the abbreviation and circle it.

For example, if you are attending a lecture on Freud, you can write:

> *(Freud) the first time you hear his name*
> *and abbreviate it as (F) each subsequent time.*

To avoid confusion, you may sometimes want to use two or even three letters as an abbreviation. This can particularly help if the key term itself is made up of several terms. For example:

> *Gross National Product can be abbreviated (GNP.)*
> *The Trojan War might be abbreviated (TW.)*

> Develop your own shorthand for taking notes quickly.
> Just make certain your notes make sense to you.

Using two or three letters can also help avoid confusion between terms that start with the same letter. For example, you can distinguish Dickens from Darwin within the same lecture as:

DK and *DW*

In addition to using capital letters and initials, you can also abbreviate longer words by making them shorter. If a word or name has several syllables, you can use just the first syllable or two instead of writing out the entire word. For example:

the term autobiography can be abbreviated autobio.

Use Signs and Symbols.   It can also make note taking much easier if you use signs and symbols for certain commonly repeated words. Again, the idea is to keep it simple. Don't fill up your notes with so many signs that they become impossible to read. Settle on a few common signs that you understand and use all the time. That way, when you read over your notes, you'll know what the signs mean right away without having to think about it.

Here are some suggestions for common symbols to help with your note taking. You can use these or come up with your own.

+   in addition, and

=   equals, is the same thing, is defined as

≠   is not the same thing, is different, unequal

i̇e   for example

≈   approximately

↗   increases

↘   decreases

∿↗   has an affect or influence on

⟶   leads to, results in

@   at or about

✳ or !   this is an important point

VS.   compared to

— —   indicates a new point being raised

;   indicates a closely related point

( )   indicates additional information or a description of a point

(?)   I'm confused about this and need to double-check it

The last sign is very important, as it signals a problem and alerts you that you need to get more information. Using this circled question mark, you can go on with your note taking without worry. The important thing is not to get stuck on the confusing points — there'll be time to get clarification later, outside of class. Make certain to put the question mark in a circle so that you can distinguish it from other question marks.

Draw Charts and Diagrams.   A picture paints a thousand words and, when it comes to taking notes, drawing a picture is quicker and more concise than writing a detailed explanation. You might, therefore, want to sketch charts and diagrams whenever possible. You don't need to be Picasso to draw a quick, easy-to-read sketch that conveys important information. Just don't overdo it; the purpose of including charts and diagrams is to save time and make your notes easier to understand.

If a particular term or concept lends itself to a simple diagram or chart, you should include it. Charts are particularly effective at indicating relationships among terms, people, and concepts. For example, if your professor is telling you about the British royal family, it is much easier to sketch a small family tree that indicates the family's relationships than to continue writing "and Henry married Eleanor and their children were Henry, Edward, and Mathilda, and they married . . . . " Charts are also effective when a professor is comparing and contrasting various concepts. You can align the concepts side by side in your notebook to show how they differ.

Drawing a diagram is an effective way to provide a fast visual description of something that might take many sentences to describe. To describe the components of a neuron, for example, you'd have to write all this:

> A neuron is made up of three key subdivisions: the dendrites, cell body, and axon. The cell body looks somewhat like an eye, with a nucleus at the center. The dendrites branch off from the cell body, some-times quite extensively, like the branches of a tree without the leaves. The axon extends from the cell body, much like the trunk of a tree. Very often the end of the axon forks into several branches known as ter-minal endings.

Instead of writing all that, you can simply include this diagram:

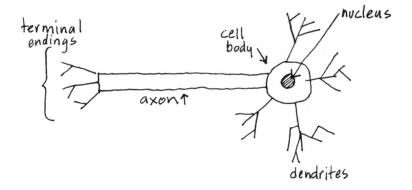

Practice.   As an exercise, go back to the lecture on Freud and take out your list of key terms. Try now to include a brief definition of each key term using the shorthand described here (or whatever signs and symbols you prefer). The next page shows how the notes from the previous exercise look when we include brief definitions and explanations with the key terms using the shorthand. How does your list of brief definitions compare?

1. _____

2. _____

3. _____

4. _____

5. _____

6. _____

7. _____

8. _____

9. _____

10. _____

11. _____

Sample Lecture Notes with Definitions

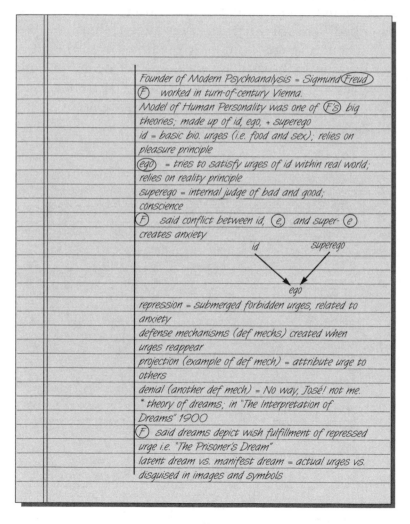

Founder of Modern Psychoanalysis = Sigmund (Freud)

(F) worked in turn-of-century Vienna.

Model of Human Personality was one of (F's) big theories; made up of id, ego, + superego

id = basic bio. urges (i.e. food and sex); relies on pleasure principle

(ego) = tries to satisfy urges of id within real world; relies on reality principle

superego = internal judge of bad and good; conscience

(F) said conflict between id, (e) and super- (e) creates anxiety

          id   superego

                    ego

repression = submerged forbidden urges, related to anxiety

defense mechanisms (def mechs) created when urges reappear

projection (example of def mech) = attribute urge to others

denial (another def mech) = No way, José! not me.

* theory of dreams; in "The Interpretation of Dreams" 1900

(F) said dreams depict wish fulfillment of repressed urge i.e. "The Prisoner's Dream"

latent dream vs. manifest dream = actual urges vs. disguised in images and symbols

4. Construct a Rough Outline

The key terms we've been discussing don't exist in isolation; instead, they are part of a larger structure that is the professor's lecture or the subject for that day's class. Each term ties in to some bigger topic or point being addressed. As you take them down, you can begin to construct a rough outline that will help you see how various terms are related and the topics they refer to.

Don't get stressed out at the idea of making an outline. You may be thinking that outlines are real headaches, that they are overly complicated and don't help all that much. The reason you feel that way is probably because you've been taught that there's only one way to make an outline and that it's a complex matter, with Roman numerals and letters. You don't have to worry about any of that. When we talk about making a rough outline for your notes, we are talking about a simple diagram that helps you to keep track of how various points and topics are related.

Before we do that, though, it will help if we look at how many teachers' lectures are structured.

What's in a Lecture?   In most cases, a lecture will focus on a *main topic*. At the start of the class, you should already have a general idea what this is. Professors who give out a syllabus or schedule of classes usually list the topic with a date. If you've gotten a schedule, make sure to look up what your teacher has planned for each day. The day's required reading can also give you a sense of what the lecture topic will be.

Knowing the main topic is an important factor. Within that main topic, there will be several additional topics your professor wants to address or points she wants to make. As you take notes, remember that each new piece of information somehow fits in with the main topic. Some pieces may be central to the topic, while others may be less important. In your outline, indicate those that are more central to the main topic.

For example, if that day's lecture concerns a particular novel, the various topics might be the characters, plot, style, and author's background. Look at the following example of a typical literature lecture:

MAIN TOPIC: A Novel

TOPIC: The Characters
   — *SUBTOPIC: Specific Characters*

TOPIC: The Plot
   — *SUBTOPIC: Various Elements of the Plot*
     — *SUB-SUBTOPIC: The Climax*

TOPIC: The Author
   — *SUBTOPIC: Childhood and Teen Years*
   — *SUBTOPIC: Early Works*
     — *SUB-SUBTOPIC: Specific Works*
     — *SUB-SUBTOPIC: Critical Reaction*

As you can see, a number of subtopics may be addressed as well. These say something specific about each of the topics.

Very often, subtopics will be examples that illustrate some major concept or principle. In a science or psychology class, for example, your professor might discuss different lab experiments that prove (or disprove) some theory.

Make a Rough Outline in Your Notes. The key terms we've been talking about all somehow fit into this structure. Some might tie into topics, others into subtopics or sub-subtopics. Getting a sense of how these terms relate to one another is an important way of understanding them. It's a good idea, as you list the key terms, to indicate how they are related by constructing a rough outline. You can try to do this in class during the lecture or when you work on your notes at home — whichever is easier for you.

For the outline, you need to group terms together so that you can see how they relate to one another and fall within specific topics and sub-topics. The best way to do this is by skipping lines between topics, and indenting terms beneath the blank lines to show that those terms are part of that topic.

Write a headline that describes each new topic in a few words, and underline it. Write in key terms as they come up by indenting them, about an inch in from the left-hand margin, beneath the topic heading. Doing so indicates the term is a part of the term above it. You can keep indenting as much as you like to indicate various subtopics and sub-subtopics. In general, the more you indent a term from the margin, the less important it is relative to the main topic.

Here is how a rough outline, without any Roman numerals or letters, might look for a typical lecture:

<u>MAIN TOPIC OF THE LECTURE</u>
(centered and underlined at top)

<u>TOPIC A *(The first topic the teacher raises)*</u>
— *Subtopic of Topic A (a discussion or term related to this first topic, but not really a totally new topic)*
— *Another Subtopic of Topic A*

<u>TOPIC B *(The next topic the teacher raises)*</u>
— *Subtopic of Topic B*
  — *A Sub-Subtopic of B (a discussion of some term or topic only related to subtopic B)*
  — *Another Sub-Subtopic of B*

One reason students get nervous taking notes is that they think the professor has some specific outline in her own notes that they need to replicate exactly. It may be true that she does have such an outline, but you don't have to imitate it. The important thing is to take notes that make sense to you. Remember, It's a *Rough* Outline and It's *Your* Rough Outline.

A good professor will make the organization of the lecture very clear, identifying new topics and important points,

Maintain a sense of the overall topic of each lecture and note general themes.

as well as the examples and subpoints. When the professor lectures, it's easy to take neatly organized notes in rough outline form. You just write down topics and terms in the order the professor introduces them.

However, not all professors are organized lecturers. Many will stray from whatever the topic is or whatever point they are making to discuss something else. This is known as a *digression*. When a professor digresses, just keep taking notes, but put them in parentheses to indicate they are digressive.

Some professors ramble on, without any clear organization to their points. They may fail to identify new topics, and jump back and forth randomly between points. In these cases, do the best you can. Keep taking notes and don't worry about keeping an outline. Try to see connections and relationships between various topics and key terms, and indicate them where you can in your notes. The thing to keep in mind is that this is just a rough sketch. Later, in stage two, you'll have plenty of opportunity to change your notes as much as you like.

Here's something else that should put your mind at ease: You don't necessarily have to have a rough outline at all! Your priority is still to get down the key terms. However, if making an outline is too much to worry about

Sample Rough Outline Notes

SIGMUND FREUD'S THEORY OF PERSONALITY

Freud
—Founder of modern psychoanalysis
—Worked in turn-of-century Vienna
—Influential and controversial figure

Model of Human Personality = one of (F's)
big theories
—Id = basic bio. urges (i.e, food and sex)
    —relies on pleasure principle; desire for
      instant gratification

—Ego = satisfies urges of id within real
   world
    —relies on reality principle

—Superego = internal judge of bad and
   good = conscience
— (Diagram: forces in conflict):

The id and superego try to influence the
ego:

      id   superego

         ego

Sample Rough Outline Notes

SIGMUND FREUD'S THEORY OF PERSONALITY (cont.)

Conflict and Anxiety
— (F) said conflict between id, (e,) and
  super(e) creates anxiety
— Repression = submerging forbidden
  urges
— Defense mechanisms created when
  urges reappear
— Types of Def Mechs:
    — Projection = attribute urge to
      others
    — Denial = No way, José! Not me.

* (F's) Theory of Dreams
— The Interpretation of Dreams (1900)
— F. said dreams depict wish fulfillment
  of repressed urges
                  (i.e., "The Prisoner's Dream")
— latent dream vs. manifest dream
    actual urges   urges disguised in
                         images, symbols
    not experienced   actually experienced
                         by dreamer
              GENERAL THEMES:
• Freud was a very influential but
  controversial figure
• Urges of the id are very powerful;
  can create anxiety
• Dreams are complex; more than meets
  the eye

in one lecture, don't. The important thing is to get those key terms down. Later on, in stage two, you'll have more time to construct an outline.

The previous pages show how a rough outline for the psychology notes we've been taking would look.

5. Note General Themes

As we have just noted, each lecture has a main topic and various subtopics. There might also be certain points, issues, and concepts that come up again and again within a single class and throughout the term. These are probably very important and should be noted.

It is also important that, at the end of each class, you take a few moments to jot down the major themes — the major topics and key points your professor made — from that day's lecture. Write these down as soon after the lecture has ended as possible, when the lecture is still fresh in your mind. Keeping track of these helps a great deal in preparation for exams. As a semester progresses, you'll begin to notice patterns in the lectures as certain themes recur. Very often, these themes are the major focus of examinations.

Ask yourself these questions: What were the major points the teacher made? What were the main topics? Try to pay particular attention to any opinions or stances about the material your professor might have conveyed to you. What seems to be the professor's personal opinion about the material? What does the professor seem to care the most about? Following are a few tricks to figuring out what the most important points are within any given lecture.

Note What's Repeated. Anything your professor says more than once is going to be important or it wouldn't be worth repeating. Make certain you put a star next to it and/or underline it, to signal that this is a very important point.

Watch Body Language/Listen for Tone of Voice. As they speak, people convey a great deal through their body language and tone of voice. Watch and listen carefully to your professors to see what additional information you can discover.

You'll probably notice a change in the professor's expression and tone of voice when he addresses important information; he might sound more earnest, passionate, or serious. He might also speak more slowly and more clearly to emphasize a major point. In terms of body language, he might look directly at students in the class rather than at his notes or the blackboard. In time, you can recognize specific actions. Many teachers take off their glasses, for example, to emphasize a key point. As you get to know your professor better, you'll become more adept at picking up these subtle clues.

Focus on Endings and Beginnings. The end of a lecture is the most important few minutes; this is when most professors will re-emphasize the main points. Sometimes, they will do this even as class is ending and students are rustling around with their books and belongings and walking out. Don't be one of those students who walks out of class immediately when time is up. For one thing, it's rude to the professor and makes a bad impression; but most importantly, you risk missing the most crucial information of the day. Be sure to write down the concluding remarks as carefully as you can.

Many professors also make key points at the start of the lecture, when they sum up points from the previous class and introduce the topic for that day. Make certain you arrive in class on time and pay special attention to what the professor says at the start. Throughout any lecture, listen for specific phrases and terms such as "to sum up," "in conclusion," "most especially," and "therefore," that indicate a professor is emphasizing a major point.

Practice. Go back to the notes you've been compiling on Freud from the sample lecture. What might be some of the general themes of that lecture? Try to write down at least three below, and then compare yours with the themes given above.

1. _____

2. _____

3. _____

Taking Notes on Seminars and Discussions

Until now, we've primarily been addressing how to take notes during a lecture, where most of the time is spent listening to the professor speaking, imparting information. Besides lectures, your classes might be seminars, where

SAMPLE NOTES OF GENERAL THEMES

Some general themes of the lecture on Freud might be:

- Freud was a very influential but controversial figure
- Urges of the id are very powerful; can create anxiety
- Dreams are complex; more than meets the eye

What did you come up with?

students participate in discussions with the professor. Discussions can sometimes happen before, after, or during a lecture, as well.

In taking notes during seminars or discussions, your concerns are somewhat different from lectures. Discussions in seminars are less oriented toward key terms and are much less structured. Here are some suggestions.

Listen More/Write Less
Since the discussion will be open, you can feel free to sit back and listen more. By following the discussion carefully, you'll learn a great deal; but it won't necessarily be important for you to document everything that is said.

Continue to Look for Key Terms
Even in a discussion, key terms may come up. You can feel comfortable sitting back and listening, but watch out for

them. Whenever the professor introduces new terms, be sure to write them down.

Note Topics, Not Opinions

Rather than write down everything that everyone says, note only the various topics that come up for discussion. What some other student thinks or feels about a given topic may help you understand the subject better, but you don't need to keep track of it in your notebook. No professor is going to test you on what another student thinks. However, having a record of the various topics that were covered in the seminar can give you a good sense of the kinds of things you'll be asked to discuss on an exam. By the way, if a student makes a particularly good or important point, the professor will probably repeat it to make certain that everyone in the class has heard and understands it. In that case, you should make some kind of note of it in your notes.

Note the Professor's Views

Your fellow students' opinions about material may not help on an exam, but your professor's views certainly might. After all, the professor is the one who makes the exams. Knowing how she thinks or feels about a topic can indicate what to emphasize in your preparation. When the professor speaks, listen to what she says and take notes. If the professor is expressing an opinion, just write, "Prof. thinks . . . . "

Some classes will mix lecture with open discussion. The professor might lecture for a while and then pose questions to the class that invite discussion. Just remember to write down what will be most important for you to know later on — key terms (with brief definitions) and general themes — at whatever point in the class in which they come up. Pay attention particularly to whatever the professor says during lecture or discussion, and write down notes on any new information.

More to Come

What we've been discussing so far is how to take good notes while you are in class. Many students think that this is all they need to do when it comes to taking notes. However, if you just take notes in class and then forget about them until an exam, you're not really absorbing the information that you wrote about. Even more of a problem, you risk discovering too late that your notes are incomplete or confusing. A real secret to study success is working on the notes you take *inside* the classroom, *outside* the classroom. We'll look at how to do that in the next section on study secrets for outside the classroom.

Study Tips:
Outside the Classroom

As a student, much of your time will of course be spent inside the classroom. However, the most intense and challenging work you do will take place outside the classroom, where you'll have to work on a variety of school-related tasks, assignments, and responsibilities on your own. That means it's especially crucial for you to have effective strategies you can follow to ensure that you complete all of your duties successfully and on time.

The main tasks you will need to work on outside the classroom are reading texts, preparing for exams, writing essays, and working more with your notes. You might also have other projects and homework assignments, such as problem sets for math and economics, or lab reports.

Reading skills, writing essays, and studying for tests are covered in detail in other books in the *Backpack Study Series*, where you'll also find many special study tips to help guarantee your success. In this section, though, you will find a brief description of a step-by-step strategy for each of these tasks. You'll also find a detailed discussion of how to work with your classroom notes at home.

Finding a Comfortable Study Space

Many people seem to think that the only way to study is at a bare desk, with a hard-backed chair, in some minuscule study cubicle in the library. While this setting does wipe out any outside distraction, it's such a gloomy, sterile atmosphere that it turns studying into a form of medieval torture. Studying just doesn't have to be that depressing.

Since you will spend long hours at the books, reading over your notes and assigned texts, you might as well make yourself comfortable. If you work in a space where you are relaxed and feel at home, you will study more often and more effectively. Study anywhere you feel comfortable — in your room, in bed, at the library, in an empty classroom, at a café, outside, in the park — provided that you do two things: 1) minimize outside distractions; and 2) promise yourself to make a change if you don't get the work done.

In choosing a place, consider the amount of outside distraction — such as friends stopping by, the phone ringing, loud music playing — and do what you can to minimize it. Even the library may not be distraction-free; if everyone you know goes there to study, you may spend more time chatting with friends than studying. You can, though, minimize the distraction by avoiding the main study lounge and finding a quieter section of the library, where you won't run into many people you know.

There's nothing wrong with studying in your room so long as you get work done. Your room is, after all, the space where you are most at home. However, you will need to

Find comfortable spaces in which you can study efficiently without distraction. If you aren't getting work done, find someplace else.

minimize distractions. If you are frequently interrupted by the phone, turn the ringer off; if friends frequently disturb you, keep the door closed.

If you decide to study in your room, it's a good idea to designate a spot as your main work space. Your desk is probably the best place. However, your room need not have a sterile, austere atmosphere. Since it's your room, you can personalize it by hanging up posters or photographs.

You can even listen to music while you study, just as long as it doesn't distract you. Listening to something old that you are very familiar with will distract you less than something brand new. If you study outside your room, you can bring a portable tape or CD player with headphones along and listen to relaxing music. That's one way to make wherever you study feel a little more like home.

Whatever study space you choose, try to do most of your work there. This will help make studying more of a habit. Arriving at that space — whether it's your desk in your room or your favorite spot in the library — alerts you to the fact that it is time to work. You can begin work more easily in a familiar setting than you can in a strange environment.

You can also designate different places for different study tasks. For example, you might decide to read assignments for class at home, but go over lecture notes in the library. Studying in a variety of locations does make the process less tedious. Still, you should make it a habit to do the same study tasks in the same place so they will seem more routine.

Sometimes, for whatever reason, you'll find it difficult to pay attention. When this happens, a simple change of scene may be all you need to refocus on your work. If you've been studying at your desk, go out somewhere, to a coffee shop or the library, and see if you get more done. Yet, if you find you consistently don't get a great deal of work done, make a more permanent change. For example, if you are so relaxed studying in your room that you always fall asleep, then that's not the best place for you to work.

Remember, pick a study space where you feel relaxed and comfortable, but one where you also get work done. This means being honest with yourself. Only you know whether you are studying effectively; if you aren't, then you need to make changes.

Note Taking Stage Two: Outside the Classroom

Most students don't open their notebooks again until exam time, only to find they can't make sense out of much of what they've written. This produces a last-minute panic before the exam, as they struggle to relearn an entire semester's worth of material in a few days. Instead of waiting until the last minute to figure out what you've got in your notes, you should get in the habit of working with them outside the classroom throughout the semester. What follows is a step-by-step procedure for reading over and adding to your notes to guarantee they are as complete and helpful as possible. An added bonus to working on your notes this way is that it helps you to be a more active student; rather than just taking down notes and forgetting about them, the steps outside class will help you to absorb, retain, and truly learn the information covered in your notes.

1. Read Over Your Notes

Read your notes over at least once outside of class. This will serve two very important purposes: It will give you an opportunity to clarify anything that might be confusing, and it will help you learn the information. It also helps you develop a comfortable familiarity with the whole subject.

If you continue reading your notes, you'll become more and more immersed in your subject. When the exam comes, you'll feel like you have the information well at hand. Questions won't shock you because they seem alien; instead, they will elicit more educated responses.

Make reading over your notes a part of your study habits. You don't need to spend a great deal of time doing this — one or two hours a week per subject should be plenty of time. It's a good idea to do this on Friday or the weekend, so you can look at all your notes for the week. You don't have to read over your notes each night; in fact, you're better off leaving them alone for a few days. That way, you can approach them with a fresh eye.

2. Ask Yourself Questions

Don't read over your notes passively. You won't learn anything if you simply read without thinking about what you are reading. Instead, become as involved in your notes as you can. You can do this by considering these questions as you read:

- What does this mean? Does it make sense?
- How are these terms and topics related to one another?
- How do these terms and topics fit into the big picture?

3. Take Notes on Your Notes

If you have drawn a line down each sheet of notes, you should have a blank column to the left of the margin. You can now use this space to take notes on your notes. As you ask yourself the questions just listed, jot down answers here. If something confuses you, make a note of it.

You can also begin to make connections between various topics and terms in this space. During class, you might have tried to put your notes in a rough outline form. As you read over them, other relationships might become clear. No longer in the middle of a lecture, you now have a sense of the whole topic. You know where your professor is heading with the material. You have a better sense of what information is important and what doesn't matter as much. Jot down these thoughts in that left-hand margin. Remember also that you only took notes on one side of

> Notes aren't finished when you leave the classroom. Continue working on them and thinking about them at home.

the page in class. You can use the back side now for any additional notes if you run out of room in the left-hand column.

4. Go to Other Sources

As you were reading over your notes, you should have marked areas or written down things that confuse you. Rather than letting those things go and praying they won't be on an exam, you should now take the time to figure them out.

Many people assume that the only source for information for class notes is the professor. That means you are entirely dependent on that one person for all the information. That's not fair to the professor and it's not fair to you. No one can communicate everything in a way that's entirely clear to every person. And as we've mentioned, some professors are much better at communicating than others. At the same time, you've got to take some responsibility for your own education. You can't just sit back and rely on someone else to do all the work for you.

So, if something confuses you, try to educate yourself. There are several places where you can get help, and you can usually get it quickly and easily.

Borrow a Friend's Notes. No two people take exactly the same notes. There's a good chance that something you missed during a lecture was caught by someone else. If you missed some information or don't understand a section of your notes, look at a friend's notes. There's absolutely nothing wrong with sharing notes with a friend. Just make certain the friend is a reliable note taker. You don't want to borrow notes from someone who doesn't take decent notes; you might wind up copying down incorrect information. However, if you know someone who seems to be a smart student and an efficient note taker, you can begin to exchange notes on a regular basis.

Check Your Textbook. Your textbook for the course and any other required reading materials are valuable resources. Very often, the required reading assignments you do outside of class correspond to the lectures. These may cover many of the same topics and key terms discussed in the lecture. In a lecture, your comprehension is dependent on your listening skills during a limited time period, but in a textbook, where there is a written explanation laid out on the page, you have plenty of time to try to make sense of the material.

Check the index of the textbook for a listing of the topic or key term for which you want more information. The text's discussion of it may not necessarily be in the same chapter you read for homework. By checking the index, you'll be able to see all the pages in the book where the term is mentioned. For all you know, there is an excellent definition and description of a term in a chapter that's not assigned.

You don't need to rely on what the teacher says as your only source of information. Consult other sources for additional information or to clarify points that confuse you.

Find More Sources. Sometimes the textbook may still be rather confusing and not give all the information you need. You might, therefore, want to turn to other sources. By reading someone else's explanation, you might begin to get a better understanding of the term. In general, the more explanations and interpretations you read, the more complete an understanding you gain.

You can begin by looking at other textbooks for more information. You don't have to buy another textbook, although you may want to if it will be very helpful. Many school libraries have several textbooks in the reference section. You also need not limit your research to textbooks. If you need suggestions for books and articles to examine, check your textbook to see if there is a bibliography (list of sources used in the book) or a list of suggested further reading.

You can also check the subject catalog at the library for other books on that topic. You don't necessarily have to go in search of a specific source; you can simply go to the section of the library where that particular subject is shelved and browse. You'll be amazed at the kinds of things you find. Very often you will get lucky and find a book that covers the course topics clearly and concisely. There may even be a study guide with beautifully written summaries of all the topics you're researching. As you browse, check the tables of contents and indexes for the terms you need help with. You can also go to bookstores with decent academic and scholarly sources, such as campus bookstores, and browse.

The Internet is another valuable resource for getting information. If you have access to the Internet and are comfortable using it, you might find all kinds of materials that can help increase your understanding. Use a search engine to help you find Web sites by subject.

Ask the Professor. Asking the professor for extra help — either by raising your hand in class or going to his office — might seem like the best way to get a quick and easy explanation of something that confuses you, but it isn't always. For one thing, there's no guarantee he will provide any better an explanation outside of class than he did inside of it. Another problem is that if you always rely on your professor for explanations, you give the impression that you cannot think for yourself. You don't want a professor to have that picture of you in mind when he assigns your grade.

If you are having real trouble understanding an important issue, feel free to go see the professor during office hours. In fact, going to see your professor a few times a semester is a good idea. That way the professor gets to know you by name and you give the impression of being a student who cares about the subject and your education. Just don't overdo it.

5. Fill in Additional Information

As you go about your additional research, make sure you take notes and fill in missing information in your notebook. If you found an explanation or definition that helps, write it in your notes. Use the space on the left side of the margin or the back of the sheet. You can also take notes on additional sheets and add them to the notes for that day's lecture in your loose-leaf notebook.

Practice.   Remember those notes you took on the sample lecture from Freud? As an exercise, take out those notes, read them over, ask yourself questions, and try to add some additional notes. The following page shows how the notes on Freud might look after a student has worked with them outside of class.

6. Rewrite Your Notes (Optional)

Some people believe in rewriting all their notes. They go home each night and do it meticulously in another notebook. That's pretty much a waste of time and paper. Rewriting doesn't help at all if you haven't really read and thought about the notes, and worked to try to understand them.

However, with the method we've been discussing, you have worked on your notes outside of class. In the process, they may have become disorganized and messy, especially as you've added information from other sources. In this case, you may want to rewrite them. You may, for example, want to incorporate the information from the left side of the margin into the notes on the right side. If you have the time, by all means go ahead and do it.

Something else might have happened in this process of re-examining and researching your notes. You may have developed a much better understanding of how various topics and terms are related. You may see that certain points go together in a certain way, while others belong somewhere else or are not very important. If this has happened, you may want to rewrite your notes with a new rough outline that makes more sense to you. This may arrange information in a very different way than your professor delivered it in class. But that's fine. The important thing is that these notes now make sense to you.

The pages show how the notes on Freud might look after you've worked on their organization and rewritten them.

Sample Lecture Notes with Additional Notes and Information

SIGMUND FREUD'S THEORY OF PERSONALITY

Definition of psycho-analysis? In Bernstein text: Therapy based of (F)'s theory of personali-ty; aims to help patient gain insight into his/her own subconscious.	Freud —Founder of modern psychoanalysis —Worked in turn-of-century Vienna —Influential and controversial figure
	<u>Model of Human Personality</u> = one of (F's) big theories —id = basic bio. urges (i.e., food and sex)

Why is (F) controversial? Cooper article says (F.) made generalizations based on a few personal, biased observations. Not scientifically <u>valid</u>. Cites several studies that disprove F's ideas.	—relies on pleasure principle; desire for
	       instant gratification
	- ego = satisfies urges <u>of</u> id <u>within</u> real
	  world
	    —relies on reality principle
	—superego = internal judge of bad and good
	  = conscience

	— (Diagram: Forces in Conflict): The id and superego try to influence the ego:

id   superego

ego

Sample Lecture Notes with Additional Notes and Information

SIGMUND FREUD'S THEORY OF PERSONALITY

How does (F.) say	Conflict and Anxiety
suppression happens?	— F said conflict between id, (e) and
Textbook discusses key	super(e) creates anxiety
role of parents who	— Repression = submerging forbidden
punish and disapprove.	urges
Other def. mechs?	— Defense mechanisms created when
	urges reappear
Other def mechs?	— Types of (Def Mechs:)
-reaction formation	— projection = attribute urge to
-displaced aggression	others
-sublimation	— denial = No way, José! Not me.
(all these are defined	
in the book)	* F's Theory of Dreams
	—The Interpretation of Dreams, 1900
	—F. said dreams depict wish fulfillment
How do dreams play	of repressed urges
into other psychologists'	(i.e. "The Prisoner's Dream")
theories?	—latent dream vs. manifest dream
I seem to remember	(actual urges (urges disguised in
Jung was into dreams.	not experienced) images, symbols
Remember to compare	actually experi-
notes on Freud with	enced by dreamer
notes on Jung!	GENERAL THEMES:
	• Freud was a very influential but
	controversial figure
	• Urges of the id are very powerful;
	can create anxiety
	• Dreams are complex; more than meets
	the eye

Sample of Rewritten, Reorganized Notes

SIGMUND FREUD'S THEORY OF PERSONALITY

<u>Freud</u> =
—Founder of modern psychoanalysis, which Bernstein defines as therapy based on (F's) theory of personality that aims to help the patient gain insight into his/her own subconscious.

    —Influential and controversial figure—Cooper article says F made generalizations based on a few personal, biased observations; not scientifically valid.

<u>Model of Human Personality</u> = Major theory of (F)
—id=basic bio. urges (i.e., food and sex); relies on pleasure principle
—ego=satisfies urges of id within real world; reality principle
—superego=internal judge of bad and good; the conscience
(*NOTE: Prof. said id + superego try to influence behavior of the ego.)

<u>Conflict and Anxiety</u>
According to F:
<u>anxiety</u>= conflict between id, e, and super-e
<u>repression</u>= submerging forbidden urges
<u>defense mechanism</u> created when urges reappear (Textbook says suppression results when parents punish/disapprove).
Types of def. mechs:
projection, denial, reaction formation, displaced aggression, sublimation

Sample of Rewritten, Reorganized Notes

SIGMUND FREUD'S THEORY OF PERSONALITY (cont.)

F's Theory of Dreams (Fr. Interpretation of Dreams, 1900)
—depict wish fulfillment of repressed urges
—latent dream   vs.   manifest dream
actual urges not experienced   urges disguised in
  symbols, images
          actually experienced by dreamer

(*NOTE: compare to notes on Jung and theory of collective
  unconscious.)

GENERAL THEMES:
* Freud was a very influential but controversial figure.
* Urges of the id are very powerful; can create anxiety.
* Dreams are complex; more than meets the eye.

Is It Cake Yet?

If you've followed the note taking methods outlined in this book, both inside and outside the classroom, you will have accomplished a great deal. Not only will you have notes that accurately represent the lecture, you'll also have begun to process the material, making it part of your general knowledge. As we'll see, this will make preparing for exams much less stressful for you than for most of your classmates.

The important thing to remember about notes, at least as we've been approaching them, is that they are never really finished products. Most students think their notes are done when the lecture is over. This thinking creates problems that come back to haunt them at exam time. These students open their notebooks and find they can't make heads or tails out of much of what they wrote. Moreover, they have to struggle to memorize their notes that they are seeing as if for the first time.

Instead of thinking of notes as finished, the method we've outlined looks at them as a continuing process. Your notes are not finished the moment class ends; instead, you add, expand, and change them to reflect new information you discover. Nothing says you can't go back to reread and add to your notes. While this should be done each week for that week's notes, you can keep going back to these notes throughout the semester. As you learn new information in lectures and reading, you may think back on previous information. You may make connections between different points from different lectures. You may also gain a greater understanding of earlier information.

This method reflects a more accurate view of how learning takes place. You don't learn by ingesting entire blocks of information in one gulp. The mind processes information over time. As you hear and read and discover new information, your mind connects it with previous information. Something that you didn't understand before may suddenly click into place. As you gain more understanding of something, you make it a part of your overall knowledge. That means it stays with you for long periods of time — right through an exam and beyond.

Reading Texts and Other Sources

Just as it's crucial to take notes and listen actively in class, you need to learn to read actively when reading required assignments for your classes. Many students think that by sitting down and reading the words on the page they somehow absorb the information. But to learn as you are reading you have to be an active reader. That means doing more than looking at the words, but thinking about the material while you read and making an effort to understand it so it becomes a part of your general knowledge.

To make reading a more active task, try applying the step-by-step strategy that follows.

> Think about the material while you read and make an effort to understand it.

Know Where You Are Headed and Why

There's always a danger while reading that your mind will wander. To help avoid that, make certain you have a goal in mind from the beginning and that you continually work your way toward that. Before you begin reading, think a bit about *what* you are reading. What is the title of the chapter, article, or text? Does it give you any hint as to what you can expect to read? As with classroom lectures, each chapter or article you read will have a main topic. Make sure you know the topic before you start to read.

Next, try to get a sense of the chapter's contents. Glance through the chapter and look at the various headings and subheadings of different sections. Look at the pictures, diagrams, and charts. Try to get a sense of what topics are included within a chapter, how they relate to one another, and how they come together within the main topic.

As you embark on your reading assignment, you'll find that keeping the "big picture" in mind will help keep you on track. As you read, you'll have a sense of how each section fits into the overall text. You'll also know how much more material you have ahead of you, which can help you plan your time. As we'll also see, gaining a sense of the chapter's contents in advance can help you read more selectively.

In addition to getting a sense of what you are reading, try to keep in mind *why* you are reading. Of course, one reason why you are reading is because it is required by your teacher. But if that is the only reason, you are going to get bored with it pretty quickly. Each thing you read should somehow contribute to your understanding of the course material as well as your general knowledge. If you can designate a purpose for each thing you read, you'll feel better about doing the work. You won't be reading just to please the professor, but because you see some value in fulfilling the assignment.

Think about some of these questions:

- What do you think your professor is hoping you will gain by reading this?
- How does the chapter or text fit in with the overall subject matter of the course?
- How does the chapter or text fit in with the lectures for that week?
- Does the chapter build on previous material from the course? How?
- Does the chapter prepare you for upcoming topics? How?
- Is anything in the chapter familiar to you (either from the course or from other classes and personal experiences)? What? Where and when did you first learn about this? What did you learn already? What in the chapter is new to you?

Thinking about these questions will help you become actively involved in the reading assignment right from the start. Contemplating these issues helps you evaluate how important the assignment is to you, which will also help you be a selective reader. These questions also help you gain a more personal interest in the reading by connecting it with your overall knowledge. That way, you won't feel you are reading just because it's required, but because it can somehow enhance your understanding of the subject matter.

Make a Rough Outline

Just as you do when taking notes during a lecture, you should also make a rough outline of all reading assignments. This will fulfill two important purposes. First, taking notes will give you something to *do* while you read, making you more of an active reader with a purpose. This, in turn, will keep you focused on the assignment and minimize the tendency to let your mind wander. Second, these outlines will help you remember the material covered in the chapter. That way, when it comes time to study for an exam, you can read over these notes rather than have to go over large, highlighted chunks of text.

To make a rough outline of a reading assignment, you merely need to note the various topics and subtopics covered in the chapter. You'll find that making an outline for a reading assignment will be easier than taking notes during a classroom lecture. Most textbooks, unlike most professors, make it very clear how they are organized. Many books will list (either in the table of contents or at the start of the chapter beneath the title) the topics covered in a particular chapter. Within a chapter, the topics, subtopics and sub-subtopics will usually be listed with clearly labeled headings and subheadings. Most books will differentiate between the more important topics and the lesser important ones by changing the style of the typeface of the headings. For example, the more important headings might be larger and/or in boldface, while lesser important ones will be smaller and in lighter or italic type.

As you read, you can watch out for headings and subheadings in a chapter. As they come up, write them down on the loose-leaf paper. As with any outline, the less important a topic is, the more you indent it on your paper.

Watch for the Key Terms

In the last section, we saw that most lectures center on key terms. As in classroom lectures, most textbook chapters also center on key terms — names, dates, facts, theories, and concepts — that are new to you. And just like taking notes in lectures, you should, as you read an assignment, look for the key terms and include them in your notes. It will probably be easier to identify key terms in textbooks than it is during lectures. Most textbooks put key terms in boldface or italics so you can spot them easily.

As you read the chapter and come across key terms, be sure you write them down in your notes. Try to fit them into your rough outline by placing them beneath the same heading or subheading in your notes as they appear in the chapter.

As with lecture notes, you should also try to include brief definitions of the key terms. You don't need to write definitions in complete sentences. Use the same shorthand you would for taking lecture notes. Don't copy down the exact, word-for-word explanation of the term as you find it in the text. Instead, use your own words to define the term as briefly as possible. If, as you read over your notes later on, you don't understand something you wrote, you can always refer to the textbook and reread the original explanation.

Note General Themes

When you are finished with a chapter, you should take a few minutes, (as you do after a classroom lecture), to jot down the chapter's general themes. To help you identify these themes, you might want to think back on what you've read and consider these questions:

- What seemed to be the author's main concerns in this chapter?
- What ideas, topics, or points were mentioned more than once?
- Was there any kind of introduction or conclusion in the chapter? If so, what points did the author make here?
- Did you get a sense of the author's opinion or stance on the material he or she was addressing in the chapter? What was it?

Whenever you finish a reading assignment, make sure you take a few minutes to write down a short list of the themes you encountered in the chapter. These notes will be instrumental in helping you prepare for exams. In addition to helping you recall the overall content of a reading assignment, these notes will enable you to compare the key themes of all the reading assignments and classroom lectures. This will help you gain a sense of how various parts of the course fit together. And it's a safe bet that when themes show up throughout the semester, they're important concepts likely to appear on an exam.

Write a Response

In the last chapter, we saw that effective note taking doesn't end when you leave the classroom. By the same token, the reading process doesn't have to end when you get to the last word of the chapter. If you want to learn something from what you've read, it is crucial that you *think* about it after you've finished reading. An excellent way to keep you thinking about what you've read is to write a *reading response*.

To write a reading response, you simply write whatever you want to about what you've read. First, close the book and put it aside, and take out a few sheets of fresh paper. As you did when taking notes in class, you should draw a line down the page so that you have a left-hand margin of about three inches. Write your response only on the right side of the margin; you'll use the space on the left-hand side later on. Then start writing.

A reading response is *not* a summary of the chapter. Instead, it's your opportunity to engage with the material you've just read. Think of yourself as having a conversation with the text, or perhaps with the author of the text. This is your chance to share whatever is on your mind in response to what this other person has just told you.

Here are some of the questions you might address in your response:

- What was your emotional reaction to what you've read. Did you like what you read? Why or why not? How did reading the text make you feel? How do you think the writer wants you to feel?
- What points do you think were most important to the writer? Did the writer successfully convey these points to you?
- What parts, if any, did you have trouble understanding? Why? What made it confusing?
- What questions about the text do you still have? In the response, you should list as many questions about the chapter as you can possibly think of. Be sure to include questions about any terms, topics, or points you didn't understand. You can also list questions you have that arise from what you have read. What additional questions about the subject matter do you have that were not addressed in the text?

These questions don't necessarily have to be answered right away. They may be answered as you read more throughout the semester — or they may never be answered. But

Think about how this text connects with other things you've learned. Does it tie into things you've studied in other courses? Does the reading remind you of anything else you have learned or experienced?

either way, asking questions gets you thinking about what you read and makes you more responsive to the material.

These are just some suggestions of topics you can address in your response. But you can feel free to write about anything you want, just as long as it is in direct response to the reading. Set a specific amount of time during which you will write about the assignment without stopping. You can set a limit of about five or ten minutes per assignment. Or you might set a page limit of one or two pages of response for every five you read. It's up to you how you do this; just make certain you always write some kind of response.

Follow Up

Once a week, set aside time to read over your responses to all the reading assignments for the previous week. Pay special attention to any questions you had about things that you did not understand and make a note of them in the space you left on the left-hand side of the margin. As you did with your notes from lectures, you can then go to other sources for more detailed explanations of these tricky concepts. Use the left-hand column to take notes from these other sources.

Follow organized, step-by-step strategies outlined here (and discussed in detail in other books in the Backpack Study Series) to work outside of class effectively, efficiently, and *actively*.

You may want to read over these responses throughout the semester, especially as you get closer to an exam. You'll find that as a course progresses and you get deeper into the subject matter, you'll gain a better understanding of key concepts. You'll also start to see how different concepts are related to one another and how they fit into the "big picture" of the overall course. A reading assignment that initially confused you may make much more sense later in the semester. Long after you've completed a reading, you might begin to see how the material relates to another reading or topic covered in class. You can then go back over your initial response and make notes in the left-hand column that indicate what you now understand about the reading.

Writing Essays

Writing essays and working on other written assignments are the primary ways in which you communicate to your professor what you understand, think, feel, or believe about a given subject. To communicate your ideas in a way that shows them off to their advantage, this step-by-step strategy is recommended.

1. Choose a General Topic

To choose a topic, take into account the nature of the assignment and its requirements. Some teachers leave you tremendous choice, while others provide very strict requirements and limitations. Make certain you know the teacher's expectations and keep those in mind even when choosing the topic. Consider the page requirements and try to choose a topic that you can discuss fully and in detail within that space. Also try to choose something that interests you personally; this will make the entire process less tedious.

The topic at this point can be somewhat generalized. As you research and think about it, you'll be able to narrow it down to a more specific thesis statement. A good starting place for a general topic might be a work of literature, an author, a historical period or news event, a scientific field or subfield, or a particular historical or social issue.

2. Read, Think, Percolate

After choosing the general topic, immerse yourself in it by reading and thinking about it at greater length. This will help you learn more about the subject and generate your own unique ideas about it. It will also help you narrow down the general topic to a more specific thesis statement.

3. Design a Thesis Statement

A thesis is the paper's central idea; it functions as the essay's backbone, holding the various parts of the essay together as a cohesive whole. The thesis, more specific than the general topic, should reflect a point of view or argument about the topic. This is condensed into a single sentence that sums up the central idea or argument of the essay. A thesis statement should be specific, reflect your own ideas and opinions, and be something around which you can build a solid supporting argument.

4. Conduct Research

Many essays for school will require conducting research using outside sources. To find sources, your best bet is to go to a library and look in subject catalogs and at bibliographies and other indexes. Once you have a list of possible sources, track them down and begin reading them and taking notes on them. For every source you find, make a bibliography card detailing the publication information.

5. Take Notes

While reading the sources, take notes on index cards. Each card should have one specific piece of information that supports your thesis statement. You can also take notes on anything that relates to your general topic, in case you need these while you are writing. Take notes carefully, either quoting directly from the source or paraphrasing (summing up main points in your own words).

6. Jot Down Your Own Ideas

In addition to information you get from sources, your own ideas also have an important place in the essay. As you go about this entire process of researching and writing an essay, you'll continually be generating your own ideas. Be sure to keep notes on these as well so that you won't forget about them. You can then use them as you write the essay.

7. Organize Your Notes and Plan an Attack

When you are done conducting research and taking notes, read over all your note cards. Toss out any that don't apply to your thesis or topic. Try to regroup the rest into categories of similar ideas. Then write a rough outline in which you list these topics in the approximate order in which you will discuss them in the essay. As you do this, think about what will make the most convincing and effective argument in support of your thesis.

8. Use a Three-Part Essay Structure

A three-part essay structure made up of the introduction, body, and conclusion ensures the essay remains focused on a specific point and that ideas are represented in a logical and organized fashion. As you start drafting your essay, follow this format. The introduction, the first paragraph in the essay, introduces your general topic and leads up to the specific thesis statement. The body is the bulk of the essay, in which you present your detailed argument that supports the thesis statement. The conclusion, the last paragraph, asserts that the thesis has been proven, summarizes key points from the essay, and may raise a new idea or question.

9. Write and Revise in Several Drafts

You can begin writing with very rough drafts in which you attempt to get on paper (or on your computer) your main ideas and notes from your research, following the three-part structure and your outline. In early drafts, you don't need to worry about grammar or style; just concentrate on getting all the information on paper. As you revise the essay, you can fine-tune it and make improvements.

As you read over your drafts, ask yourself questions about what you see on the page:

- Is everything explained fully?
- Will the reader understand everything as it is currently explained here?
- Are there any holes or gaps in the argument?
- Are any ideas not fully developed or only partially explained?
- Does one idea flow smoothly into the next?
- What additional information does the reader need to appreciate this point?

As you read the draft, sit with a pen in your hand and make notes. Try to anticipate specific questions a reader might have about what is on the page and write them down in the margins. After you've read over the draft and made notes on it, then go back to the beginning and revise it. As you revise, include more information that answers those questions a reader might have when reading the essay.

You should continue to reread and revise the essay as many times as necessary until you are satisfied with it. Each time you redraft, you make changes to improve the essay.

The first few times you read and rewrite, you should focus on the content — the ideas and points that are explained in the essay. Make certain all your ideas are clearly and fully explained, that nothing is ambiguous or partially stated, and that there are no gaps in the discussion. Examine the overall organization of the essay and make sure that one point flows smoothly and logically into the next. You might try moving sections of the essay around to see if they work more effectively and strategically somewhere else. Check that everything in the essay supports the thesis statement, and take out anything that detracts from the argument.

In later revisions, you can concentrate less on the content and more on the writing itself. Read through the essay and pay attention to how things are phrased. Work on individual paragraphs and sentences to ensure they are well-written and flow together. Think about ways you might rephrase or reword various sentences to make them clearer or more effective.

If working with information from other sources, be sure to cite that information carefully and in the proper format. Ask your teacher what format to follow for citations. In general, make certain every piece of information from an outside source is indicated as such in the essay. You also need to include a bibliography of works cited at the end of the essay with the full publication information for each source you use.

10. Edit and Proofread Carefully

When you are satisfied with the essay, you need to proofread the final version very carefully. Look for any spelling or grammatical errors, and double-check your citations. You want the final version of the essay to be virtually flawless; this indicates to the teacher that you take your work seriously. Make certain the final version is typed neatly, stapled, and includes a title and your name.

Preparing for Exams

On exams, you are expected to communicate to your teacher what you have learned in the course and understand about the subject. There are many different kinds of exams that combine various kinds of questions. The main types of questions are short answers (such as multiple choice or fill in the blank), problem solving (such as math problems), or written responses (such as short or long essays). To prepare for exams, you need to review all of your materials and notes from throughout the semester and absorb as much as possible. It's not only an issue of memorizing everything (although memorizing terms and facts is an element of test preparation), but of understanding concepts and ideas that you can apply to different questions.

To help prepare for exams in an organized, efficient, and active manner, you can use the following step-by-step strategy.

1. Read Over All Notes from Class Lectures and Readings

Before you begin studying for an upcoming exam, gather together all of your notes from the course — notes from class and from your readings — in one binder. This should not be a problem since you've been putting your notes in a binder at home throughout the semester. Just make sure you now have them all in one place, in a logical order.

The first step in the process is to read these notes from start to finish. It is extremely important that you do this in one sitting *without interruption*. This will help you concentrate more intently on the material; more importantly, it will enable you to develop a clear picture in your mind of the course material as a whole. Rather than studying various bits and pieces of information related to the subject, you'll now be able to see how everything fits together as part of the overall course.

For each examination, set aside several hours to read through your notes from beginning to end. However, don't study several subjects at once or one subject right after another. If you study several courses within a short period of time, the material can easily become mixed up and muddled in your mind, making it more difficult for you to remember specific details. Make certain you take a break of at least two hours before sitting down to read notes from another course.

2. Create Master-Lists from Notes.

As you read over your notes from classroom lectures and reading assignments, you are now going to condense and reorganize the material onto three single sheets of paper — the three Master-Lists. The preparation of these lists is itself a part of the study process; by reorganizing material from the course, you gain a firmer grasp on the subject. At the same time, the Master-Lists serve as study tools; rather than having to read through all of your notes again and again, you only need to study these three sheets. Each Master-List prepares you for a specific kind of examination question.

The Master-List of Key Terms.   If you've been following the methods for note taking described in this book, then you have been listing key terms in outline form every time you took notes on classroom lectures and reading assignments. As part of your exam preparation, you now create a Master-List of Key Terms from those notes. As you read through all your notes, write down the key terms — that means any names, dates, concepts, or ideas that are new to you and/or central to the course — without any definition or explanation of them. You can also use the Master-List of Key Terms to list any formulas or principles you need for problem solving.

Try to squeeze all the key terms onto a single sheet of paper. Don't write down any of the terms more than once; if a key term came up repeatedly throughout the course, you only need to write it down once on your Master-List. You may also decide to eliminate some key terms from the Master-List because you realize, in retrospect, that they aren't all that important.

The Master-List of General Themes. As you've been taking notes throughout the semester, in addition to writing down key terms you've also been noting the general themes of each lecture and reading assignment. As you prepare for an exam and read through all of your notes, you should now create a Master-List of General Themes. As with the Master-List of Key Terms, you want to squeeze all of the general themes onto a single sheet of paper. If a particular theme recurred throughout the course, you don't need to write it down more than once on the Master-List. However, you should put a star beside any recurring theme to indicate its importance.

The Master-List of Related Concepts. Creating this particular Master-List is a bit more complicated and will likely take more thought and effort than the other two. However, it will prove especially helpful in preparing for examination questions of all kinds.

As you read through your notes, try to identify groups of concepts that relate closely to one another. If you've identified such a group, write it down on the Master-List of Related Concepts and give it a subject heading.

A common category of related concepts is a principle or idea and the various examples that illustrate or support it. Ways to group related concepts together that you might include on your Master-List include:

- Events and Causes (that lead up to them)
- Rules and Exceptions

- Similar Ideas, Concepts, Theories, and Examples
- Opposite or Dissimilar Ideas, Concepts, Theories, and Examples
- Chronologies/Datelines
- Causes and Effects

Try to identify and write down as many of these groups of related concepts as you can. However, don't feel you have to identify every single one. There are any number of ways to organize ideas and you won't likely be able to pick up on each and every one. However, the process of reorganizing your notes this way encourages you to think using the same kind of logic behind most examination questions.

You might have trouble, at first, fitting all of the groups of related concepts you identify on a single sheet of paper. If this is the case, use more than one sheet. As you work more with the Master-List, you can make decisions about what to eliminate and eventually condense the list onto a single sheet.

3. Work with the Master-Lists and Quiz Yourself

After your initial reading of all your notes, you should now have created three separate Master-Lists: Key Terms, General Themes, and Related Concepts. The bulk of your preparation for the exam now centers on working with these Master-Lists. Each Master-List includes information that will help you answer a particular type of question.

Working with the Master-List of Key Terms. Many short answer questions, such as multiple choice, fill in the blank, and true/false questions, are specifically designed to test you on your factual knowledge, to see if you know the meaning of a particular term or something of significance about it. You can't figure out the answer to these questions using reasoning or other kinds of skills — either you know the answer or you don't.

While short answer questions might specifically test you on factual knowledge, you'll also often need to know these facts to write essays. Your primary goal in answering an essay question is to demonstrate to the professor your knowledge and mastery of the subject matter. Therefore, the more key terms you weave into an essay, the more you will impress the teacher with your knowledge.

For this reason, becoming very familiar with the key terms from the course is a crucial part of preparing for an examination. For some key terms, you'll need to give definitions to know exactly what they mean. For others, the term might be familiar, but you'll need to know something relevant *about* it in terms of its significance in the course. This is particularly the case with names of people, places, characters, and dates.

Therefore, as part of your exam preparation, you should spend a certain amount of time learning and testing yourself on the key terms. After you have completed your Master-List, quiz yourself on the terms. Go down the list and try to define or say something significant about each term. If possible, quiz yourself in private and discuss each

It is also crucial that you memorize any formulas or scientific/mathematic principles you need for problem solving. Talk to yourself; describe the kinds of problems you can solve with this information.

term out loud, as if you were explaining it to someone else in the room. This procedure ensures that you take the time to explain each term fully. Many times, you look at a term, think you know it, and skip to the next term. However, you may not really be able to define the term as easily or as clearly as you think. By talking about each term, you see exactly how much you do or don't know about it. You also begin to feel more comfortable discussing these terms at length, which can help when you write an essay response.

Ultimately, you want to be able to go down the list and confidently define each term or say something about its significance. You probably won't be able to do that on the first shot. You might find yourself unable to remember a certain term or hesitating when you try to define or describe it in detail. There are several techniques you can use to learn these key terms, including using cue cards, rewriting and reworking the list, and using special memorization techniques.

Working with the Master-List of General Themes. While the Master-List of Key Terms includes many of the specific concepts you learned in a particular course, the Master-List of General Themes documents the big ideas from

113

the course, such as major points and perspectives that were addressed repeatedly in class and your readings. While preparing for an examination, the Master-List of General Themes can give you insight into what you should study in detail; test questions almost always relate to the general themes rather than to more obscure points. You can therefore focus your studying primarily on those key terms and concepts that relate to the General Themes.

The Master-List of General Themes can also be a valuable tool in preparation for essay examinations. An essay question usually requires that you elaborate at length on some topic related to the course. An essay question must therefore be relatively broad so that a typical student in the class will be able to write a great deal about it. In other words, an essay question almost always reflects one or more general themes from the course.

When you take an essay examination in class, you are pressed for time. That's why many essay responses written by students are messy and unorganized. It's hard, after all, to come up with a detailed, focused response right on the spot. However, you've got your Master-List of General Themes which, as we've just seen, provides you with clues as to possible essay questions before the actual test. You can examine the list and try to think about possible essay questions involving each theme. You can then take the time to plan answers to these questions *before* the exam.

You don't, however, have to write an elaborate practice essay for each theme or possible question you come up with. Instead, write down each general theme on a separate piece of paper. For each one, think about how you would approach an essay question related to that theme and make a list of the specific points, topics, and ideas you would incorporate into your response. If there are any key terms that also relate to the theme, list those as well.

Several times before the exam, sit down with these sheets and, using the list of points you've written for each theme, talk your way through the essay response you would write on the exam. You don't need to write out an elaborate response for each one unless you want to. By talking out loud, you begin to feel more and more comfortable discussing these themes. You should try to do this exercise at least twice for each theme — once looking at the detailed list of points you've created and once looking at only the theme. If you can talk comfortably and at length about a general theme, you can also write an essay about it on an exam.

Of course, there's no guarantee that essay questions on the exam will reflect these themes in their original form. However, since most essay questions address broad topics, they will usually connect in some way with a general theme or themes. When you see the essay question, you can identify whichever theme(s) it relates to, and draw on the same concepts and points you previously thought about in conjunction with that general theme as you write your essay.

Working with the Master-List of Related Concepts. Many short answer questions are based on identifying some kind of relationship between different ideas and terms. For example, many multiple choice questions ask you to identify an example of some principle, theory, or idea. Sometimes you might have to do the opposite and identify the larger principle a particular example illustrates. For all these questions, you need to do more than be able to define the key terms; you need a sense of which terms go together and why. That's where the Master-List of Related Concepts comes in. By creating this list, you've begun thinking with the same logic and in the same terms as the exam questions.

The Master-List of Related Concepts is also helpful in preparing for essay questions. In the course of writing an essay, you may need to discuss a particular concept in detail. The Master-List helps you to identify the various topics and points that support a particular concept, providing you with detailed information you can include in an essay response. Moreover, by looking for the different groups of concepts from the course and identifying how they are related, you have reconceptualized your notes. Being able to rethink and reorganize different concepts indicates you have attained a certain degree of comfort and familiarity with these ideas.

The process of creating the Master-List of Related Concepts has already involved a great deal of thought and effort. Now that you've done the hard part, all you need to do with this list is read it over a few times before the exam to keep these ideas fresh in your mind. Making this list in advance means you've already done some serious thinking about these ideas, more than most students do before taking a major exam. You can enter an exam feeling confident about your ability to examine, think about, and answer complicated questions.

4. Get Help from Other Sources

In the sections on taking notes and reading texts, you saw that you can always turn to other sources for additional information or to get help if you are having trouble. Even if you have begun studying for an exam, it's still not too late to get help.

See the Professor.   When they sit down to study for a major exam, many students become confused or generally anxious about the test. In need of advice, they turn to what seems to be the most accessible and most reliable source of information — the professor. However, if you go to see a professor a few days before an exam and say, "I'm confused. I really need help. What do I do?" there's not all that much she can do for you this late in the game. Instead, if you come with a specific question, you can get specific information. If, as you are studying your notes, you come across anything that really confuses you, write down a specific question about it on a sheet of paper. Bring that sheet with you when you go to see the professor and go over the question. In addition to providing you with information you need, the professor might also offer additional hints as to the content of the upcoming exam.

It is also important that you don't rely solely on the professor as your source of help. Once the semester is over, many professors become scarce, which makes it difficult to see them just before a final exam. If you wait to begin studying until after the course has ended, you may not get an opportunity to see the professor. Even if a professor schedules office hours before an exam, there's no guarantee you'll get in to see her. After all, many other students probably have the same idea. Try your best, if you need to, to track down the professor. If you can't, though, there are other ways to get help.

Read Other Sources. An important component in the study strategies outlined in previous chapters was reading additional source materials, particularly when you had trouble understanding something from a lecture or reading assignment. If you have enough time, you can still read other sources when you are preparing for an exam. As you go over your notes and prepare the Master-Lists, you may come across terms or ideas that you still don't understand or that are not clear in your notes. You also may find that, as time has passed, you forgot important information. You can then turn to other sources or go to the library for more information.

There are many academic encyclopedias and dictionaries, for example, that include listings for the key terms

SPECIAL TIP:
READ MORE TO LEARN MORE

No matter what course you take or what you major in, a majority of a student's duties center on reading and writing. These skills play a vital part in completing assignments for classes and taking examinations. Fortunately, you improve these skills as you do them more frequently—even when you read for pleasure outside of class.

Studies have shown that reading frequently also improves one's writing abilities. The more you read, the more comfortable you feel with language. As a result, you gain more of an instinct for what is written correctly; as you write, something will simply "sound right" or "sound wrong."

In addition to reading, you might also consider keeping a journal. You can write down anything you wish in a journal—poetry, your thoughts and feelings, accounts of things you've done or accomplished, descriptions of things you've seen or overheard. You don't ever have to show the journal to anyone, so you don't have to worry about grammar or spelling. Just write whatever or however you like. If you write in a journal frequently, you'll become more comfortable writing in general, more accustomed to setting your thoughts down on paper.

you've studied in class. By consulting these sources, you can find clear and concise explanations of these points. Go to the reference section of the library and ask the librarian to suggest sources.

Even if you are not confused about a particular point, it's a good idea to read some additional sources anyway. The more sources you read about a particular subject, the more information you receive about it. And by reading about a subject in depth just before an exam, you immerse yourself in the material. You then enter the examination focused on and comfortable with that subject.

Consulting introductions to different editions of important primary texts can provide you with a great deal of additional information. For example, an introduction to a particular work of literature will often summarize the plot, describe the characters, and discuss major thematic and critical issues. Reading these introductions therefore helps you recall the work of literature in more detail, while providing additional points and ideas you might not have previously considered. You can also look for anthologies and collections that include articles and essays on a particular subject or by a certain writer. For example, an introduction to a volume of *Freud's Collected Writings* might summarize his major innovations, as well as critical reactions to and controversies surrounding them.

Reading about the same topic in several sources is a worthwhile exercise, as it shows you how the same subject can be described in different ways. This is important as examination questions will often be worded in a manner different from the way the material was originally described to you.

Other sources can also provide a variety of examples and illustrations of major principles. The more examples you read, the better you understand the idea or principle behind it. Finding additional examples can be particularly helpful in preparing for math and science examinations for which you are asked to complete various problems using different formulas. Seeing a variety of sample problems before an exam makes you better prepared to answer problems yourself; you are able to see the many different problems that relate to a particular formula or principle. You can even find sources with sample problems and solutions, so that you can practice with actual questions before the exam.

Other School Assignments and Projects

In addition to these basic study tasks, you might have a variety of specific projects and assignments for different classes, such as problem sets and lab reports. For these assignments, you can draw on a combination of the strategies discussed so far.

In general, for all of these tasks you complete at home, keep in mind the general priorities described in the first chapter:

- Set a goal and keep that big picture in mind as you work.
- Make the job as active as possible; be an active student, rather than a passive one.
- Communication — to yourself and to others — is the key to success on most school assignments and study tasks.
- Stay organized. That means getting all information and materials in advance, knowing exactly what to expect and what is expected of you, and keeping careful records and notes.
- Make this all a habit. For each type of assignment or project, develop an organized strategy that works for you and then make it a habit on future projects.

Be a Packrat

Many students are so relieved when the semester is over they throw away all their notes. That's a serious mistake. You've worked hard taking those notes. And, more importantly, you never know when you might need to refer back to them.

Many of the courses you take will interconnect, particularly those within your major or concentration. As you move on to more advanced levels, you'll find you need to refer to notes from earlier courses to refresh your memory about certain key points.

Save all of your notes and essays and, if possible, your books. You never know when something can help you in the future.

You also may take courses that seem completely unrelated to one another, only to find that some point or issue will come up that you have previously addressed. For example, you may be reading a novel in an English class that refers to specific historical events. If you've taken a history class about that period, you can read your notes and get more information about those events, which in turn can help you understand the novel. Imagine how impressed your teacher will be if, in class discussion, you can provide some of that background information.

At the end of the semester, rather than throwing away all your notes, neatly label and put them someplace safe and accessible. Consider purchasing a file cabinet to store them in. If you've been using a loose-leaf notebook (as recommended in this book), you can take the pages out of the binder and put them in a folder. That way you can reuse the binder next semester. Just make certain you label the folder with the course title and year. A file cabinet will help keep everything organized.

In addition to saving old notes, consider holding onto some of your required textbooks and other course materials. It's tempting at the end of the semester to sell all your books back to the bookstore — especially given how expensive books are these days. However, if there is any chance you will refer to a book — particularly if it was used in a course that is part of your major — it is probably worthwhile to keep it. One option is to sell only the textbooks and hold onto all other books. Textbooks tend to be more expensive than other books, and you get back a significant amount of money. Other books often bring only a fraction of the original cost (especially if they are paperbacks). If you sell a textbook but wind up having to purchase it again, you'll actually lose rather than save money!

Organizational Skills and Time Management 4

As we've noted earlier, as a student, you are going to have to juggle many tasks and responsibilities that will vary week by week, semester by semester. In this chapter, we'll discuss ways to plan out your schedule so that you can devote adequate time to all of your student responsibilities. We'll also discuss tips to help you motivate yourself to get work done when it needs to be.

Keeping Track

With all of the work you need to do as a student during a typical semester, it's all too easy to forget some assignment. That's an easy problem to avoid, though, if you simply keep careful records of everything you need to do. Before you begin classes, buy a pocket date book or calendar for keeping a record of all your responsibilities. Note the deadlines for assignments, exam dates, appointments with professors or study partners, and extracurricular activity meetings, as well as any other obligations. Get in the habit of carrying your date book around with you so you can make additions or changes at any time. For example, you might arrive at class one day and find out that the professor has decided to change the date

Stay organized. Carry around a date book to mark in appointments, meetings, due dates, and other commitments. Make changes immediately.

of the midterm exam. You can put the new date right in your calendar. That way you're certain not to forget it.

In addition to keeping careful records of your responsibilities in your date book, you should also make an effort to keep all your notes and study materials neatly organized. There's not much point in taking notes if they wind up in a crumpled pile of paper at the back of your desk. It's also a waste of time if you need to search for some book or article you need for a particular class assignment. Keep your notes clearly labeled and organized. Find a space you can designate as your study area, where you keep all the study materials — notes, textbooks, articles — that you need for the semester. That way you'll be able to quickly find anything you need.

Making a Study Schedule

Many study guides instruct you to set a rigid schedule for yourself in which each minute of each day is devoted to fulfilling a certain task. These schedules block off time for everything from study sessions to mealtimes to hours when you can sleep. But schedules like these are virtually impossible to stick to. What if, for example, you don't feel like eating dinner at exactly 6:30 on a particular night? What if you are supposed to study from 8:00 to 11:00 on

Tuesdays, but one week your professor wants you to attend a guest lecture at the same time? What if there is a really good party on a Wednesday night you want to go to, but you don't have time scheduled for it? What do you do?

Student life is far too chaotic to be squeezed into a neat, orderly schedule. Your schedule will change frequently: One week you may have a major exam or a paper due, which will require more work, while another week, you may have to devote substantial time to an extracurricular activity. Even weekly study tasks, such as reading lecture notes or assigned texts, will take different amounts of time. One week the assigned readings may be very difficult and take twelve hours to complete, while another they'll be substantially easier and only take four hours. But if you are stuck in a rigid schedule, you won't be able to make the necessary adjustments to provide the time you need.

However, you do need to have some kind of schedule so that you can keep track of what needs to be done and leave yourself enough time to do it. Instead of making a rigid schedule, you can plan a more *general* one that will allow you to make changes on a week-to-week and day-to-day basis.

This general schedule only shows those activities you do every week of the semester at the exact same times. You should make it up at the beginning of the semester, before classes have actually started. Make a chart listing days of the week at the top, and the hours of the day in a column on the left side. First, find out the meeting times of all your classes, and block off those times on the schedule. Then mark off any times you will be consistently unavailable to study; for example, those times when you are part of a club or a team, or perhaps working at a job.

Sample General Schedule

	Mon.	Tues.	Wed.	Thurs.	Fri.	Sat.	Sun.
9-10:00		English		English			
10-11:00	Psych 101		Psych 101		Psych 101		
11-12:00							
12-1:00							
1-2:00	Sociology		Sociology		Sociology		
2-3:00		Biology		Biology			
3-4:00	History		History		History		
4-5:00							
5-6:00	Gym		Gym		Gym		Gym
6-7:00							
7-8:00	Literary Magazine		Literary Magazine				
8-9:00							
9-10:00							
10-11:00							

Sample General Schedule

	Mon.	Tues.	Wed.	Thurs.	Fri.	Sat.	Sun.
9-10:00		English		English			
10-11:00	Psych 101		Psych 101		Psych 101		
11-12:00							
12-1:00							
1-2:00	Sociology		Sociology		Sociology		
2-3:00		Biology		Biology			
3-4:00	History		History		History		
4-5:00							
5-6:00	Gym		Gym		Gym		Gym
6-7:00							
7-8:00	Literary Magazine		Literary Magazine				
8-9:00							
9-10:00							
10-11:00							

= "Free" time

Create a general schedule for the entire semester in which all of your permanent responsibilities and commitments are blocked out.

After you've blocked off those hours, you'll be able to see the times each day that are "free." Those "free" times can be spent any number of ways — studying, doing work, socializing with friends, etc. It's up to you to decide how to best use those "free" times.

NOTE: "Free" times can be used to study, read required texts, do homework, eat, relax, and socialize.

Now you have a general schedule that indicates the times you have commitments and the times you are "free" in a given week. But each week presents its own specific tasks and requirements that you should plan for. At the start of each week, sit down and make a list of all the tasks that must be completed; this includes reading assignments, going over lecture notes, researching and writing essays, preparing for major exams, and working on school projects. If you have other things to do that week, include those on your list as well. For example, you may have to attend a special event or an extracurricular activity meeting.

Sample Weekly List of Tasks and Times

✔ Read articles for Psych.	Tues., Sun. Evenings (4 hrs.)
✔ Read Chapters 1-5 of Huck Finn	Mon. Evening (1–2 hrs.)
✔ Read Chapters 5-10 of Huck Finn	Wed. Evening (1–2 hrs.)
✔ Study for Bio. quiz on Thursday	Tues., Wed. Evenings
✔ Meet with group to work on Soc. project	Sun. Afternoon (4 hrs.)
✔ Read Chapter 14 for Sociology	Tues. Evening (1 hr.)
✔ Finish poem for Lit. Magazine	Mon., Wed. Nights (after 11 P.M.)
✔ Go over notes from lectures, readings	Sat. (4 hrs.)
✔ Do library research for Soc. project	Mon.–Thurs. Midday (between classes)

After you've made up your list of specific tasks for the week, go down the list and designate days and times to work on each task, making certain they are within the "free" blocks on the general schedule. You don't need to set exact times for each task; you can simply write down the day and general time you plan to spend doing it. You may, though, want to estimate how long each task will take to complete so that you block out an appropriate amount of time.

Sample Weekly Schedule with Tasks Estimated In

	Mon.	Tues.	Wed.	Thurs.	Fri.	Sat.	Sun.
9-10:00		English		English			
10-11:00	Psych 101		Psych 101		Psych 101		
11-12:00	Library Research for Soc. Project						
12-1:00							
1-2:00	Sociology		Sociology		Sociology		
2-3:00		Biology		Biology		Go Over Notes	Group Meeting for Soc. Project
3-4:00	History		History		History		
4-5:00							
5-6:00	Gym		Gym		Gym		Gym
6-7:00		Study for Bio Quiz					
7-8:00	Literary Magazine		Literary Magazine				
8-9:00		Psych Reading	Read Huck Finn				
9-10:00	Read Huck Finn						Psych Reading
10-11:00		Soc. Reading	Study Bio Quiz				

= "Free" time

132

> Each week, and perhaps even each day, list all of your tasks. For every item, try to estimate the length of time it will take to complete, and list when in the week you plan to work on it.

If you like, you can photocopy your general schedule and then, each week, put the specific tasks and times in. Keep in mind, though, that these are just estimates. Try to schedule the tasks during times when you do not have to be somewhere immediately afterward, in case you take longer than you estimate to finish the job.

During the week, work on each specific task during the time you've designated. However, don't force yourself to spend an exact amount of time on each one. Take each task as it comes; some will take more time than you anticipate, some will take less. Just be sure that by the end of the week you've fulfilled all the tasks you set for yourself.

You will have to read assigned texts and go over lecture notes every week, and you will probably want to work on those tasks during the same general times each week. For example, you may want to read assignments for a certain class on the same night each week so that it is completed before class the next day. Don't block off specific times to the minute, however, because the reading will take varying amounts of time.

On the following pages are blank forms for your schedule and lists of weekly and daily tasks. You can tear these out and photocopy them. Fill them in whenever you need them.

Weekly Schedule

	Mon.	Tues.	Wed.	Thurs.	Fri.	Sat.	Sun.
9-10:00							
10-11:00							
11-12:00							
12-1:00							
1-2:00							
2-3:00							
3-4:00							
4-5:00							
5-6:00							
6-7:00							
7-8:00							
8-9:00							
9-10:00							
10-11:00							

Weekly or Daily Tasks

Date(s)_____

Task	Day and Time to Work (Approximate Amt. of Time Necessary)
1._____	1._____(_____)
2._____	2._____(_____)
3._____	3._____(_____)
4._____	4._____(_____)
5._____	5._____(_____)
6._____	6._____(_____)
7._____	7._____(_____)
8._____	8._____(_____)
9._____	9._____(_____)
10._____	10._____(_____)

Daily Lists

In addition to making a weekly list of specific tasks, it's a good idea to make one for each day. Before you go to sleep each night, you can quickly make a list of the things you need to do the following day. You can include, in addition to study tasks, any specific errands you need to run, from doing laundry to returning books to the library. That way, you've got all your tasks in one place and you won't forget to do something. As you do each one, cross it off the list so you can see yourself making progress and feel you are accomplishing something.

Making Time for Fun

Everyone needs time away from work for fun and relaxation, and you should make sure you allow yourself plenty of time for both. Otherwise, you'll quickly become overworked, exhausted, and unhappy. Becoming involved with an extracurricular activity ensures that you regularly do something other than school work that you enjoy. For these activities, you do need to schedule in time throughout the semester. However, you also need time just to relax and socialize. For these kinds of activities, don't "schedule" in specific times. You might want to leave weekend nights free for fun, and you can indicate this on the schedule. However, if you schedule every "fun" minute, then fun becomes part of your routine and not all that enjoyable. Moreover, there are some times when you'll have much more free time for fun and relaxation than others, depending on your tasks for that week.

Make studying and completing your work your priority. When you've finished a task for that day, the remaining time is yours for fun and relaxation. It is okay, though, to schedule in some periods for fun if you do not have a heavy-duty schedule for that week.

As a student, your priority is fulfilling your study requirements, as well as commitments to extracurricular activities. These will take up a certain portion of time each week. When they are completed, any time that remains is yours to do with as you please.

For example, if you've designated Tuesday evening as the time to read for your Psychology class, you may find that you've finished the reading by 9 P.M. If you have no other tasks designated for that day, then you can do whatever you want with the remaining time. Expect to have less personal free time during weeks when you have exams or major papers and projects due. But always factor in plenty of time for sleep!

Prioritizing

There will be some weeks when you have an especially heavy workload and face a severe crunch for time. To prioritize your tasks, look at your list for the week and try to put them in order of importance. For example, completing an assignment that must be handed in or studying for a major exam are going to take priority over most other activities.

137

After identifying what is most important for that week, make certain you devote most of your time to fulfilling those tasks. If you finish them, spend the remaining time on the less important ones. If you don't get to the less important tasks, you can make up for it in later weeks when the workload is lighter. Just be certain you catch up at some point so you don't have a heavy workload right before exams.

Getting Motivated

You're not going to want to study every time you are supposed to. Nevertheless, you're going to have to motivate yourself somehow to do work even if you don't feel like it. One way to do this is to reward yourself when you accomplish specific study tasks.

Any time left after you've completed your study tasks for a particular day is your personal free time. This in itself serves as a reward to get you motivated to work. For example, if you know you want to watch television at night, you can force yourself to work efficiently during the day. Similarly, if you want to go to a party on the weekend, you'll try your hardest to get all your work done during the week. You just need to remind yourself of the fun activities waiting for you when you are finished working.

However, even with the promise of free time as a reward, you may still find it difficult to get motivated and begin working. You can provide yourself with additional

To motivate yourself to keep working, promise yourself little rewards for finishing each task.

rewards as you study. Set small goals, and reward yourself each time you fulfill them. For example, if you have several hours blocked off on Tuesday night for reading forty pages, promise yourself a snack after you've gotten halfway through the assignment. This will at least get you started.

These rewards don't need to be extravagant. A reward can simply be a short break to do something you like — getting ice cream, talking on the phone, going for a walk, listening to music, whatever. Just make certain the "reward" time is a short break lasting no more than twenty to thirty minutes.

This reward system is particularly helpful if you have to spend long hours at work, such as studying for an exam or writing a paper. If you think of yourself as slaving away for many long hours, it will be extremely difficult to motivate yourself to begin work. However, if you divide the task into several smaller ones and promise yourself a small reward at the completion of each one, it will be much easier to get started. You know then that when you sit down to work, a reward of some kind is not all that far away.

When you finish a major task, such as completing an essay or taking a final exam, it's nice to give yourself a bigger reward — a new CD or a fun evening out. These rewards will help you get through the especially difficult work periods during the school year.

No Time to Nap: Staying Awake While You Study

It might sound like a joke, but falling asleep while reading or studying is a problem that plagues many students. The need to sleep is powerful — and to fight it, you need to take equally strong measures. Here are a few important suggestions.

Get enough sleep at night. There's a simple reason why so many students fall asleep while studying, and it's not necessarily boredom. They're just tired. Of course, it's difficult when you are a student to get a good night's sleep all the time, and you shouldn't expect to. However, don't make a habit of staying up late all the time. Try as often as possible to get six to eight hours of sleep a night.

Don't get too much sleep. You might not realize it, but there is such a thing as *too much sleep*. For most people, six to eight hours of sleep a night is sufficient. If you get more sleep than your body needs, you can feel sluggish all day long.

Exercise regularly. If you exercise regularly, you'll sleep better at night and be more energized during the day. That means you'll be more focused on your classes and your studies.

Become alarmed. If you tend to fall asleep while studying, set an alarm. You can purchase an inexpensive travel clock or wristwatch equipped with an alarm and have it nearby

> Develop a routine that works for you; if your routine is not working, make changes.

while you study. The alarm should be loud enough to wake you up but quiet enough not to disturb those around you. If possible, set the alarm to go off every fifteen minutes. If you can't set it to go off regularly, set it for a specific time (such as a half-hour after you've begun studying) and continue to reset it each time it goes off.

Arrange wake-up calls or visits. If you don't trust an alarm, have a friend check on you every so often. The easiest method is to arrange to study together; that way you can both keep an eye on the other and keep each other awake. Of course, you have to be careful that you both don't fall asleep at the same time, and also that you don't spend too much time chatting. If you are studying in your room, you can have a friend or relative give you a phone call every hour or so to check up on you.

Take breathers. If you become too comfortable while studying, it's easy to fall asleep. You should plan to get up and walk around at regular intervals — preferably outside. While fresh air can do wonders for waking you up, limit your walks to just five minutes. When you return to studying, you'll feel revived and better able to focus.

Stay actively involved. The more engaged in the material you are, the less likely it is you'll succumb to sleep. Rather than just reading the words on the page, have a conversation with yourself in your mind about what you read; read a few lines and then comment on them.

Don't get too comfortable. It's important to be comfortable while you study because the more relaxed you are, the more open your mind will be. Additionally, being comfortable makes studying less tedious. However, there is such a thing as being too comfortable. If you find yourself constantly falling asleep, you should change your study habits. For example, if you study on a couch or bed, you might need to sit at a desk, where it is more difficult to fall asleep. If you listen to music, you might need to change your selection to something that will keep you up rather than lull you to sleep. Remember, study in an atmosphere you feel relaxed in, but not so much so that you cannot stay awake.

Go with the Tide, Not Against It

Some guidebooks claim there are optimum times and places for studying, and that all students should follow the same schedule. But not all students are alike. One might be a morning person who works most efficiently in the early hours, while another is a night owl, whose best work is produced after midnight. One might study efficiently in the library, while another works best lying on the couch in the dorm lounge. It's therefore foolish to think all students should study in exactly the same way, according to the same schedule. In fact, forcing yourself to follow a schedule that doesn't suit your personality makes the process less effective and much more tedious than it needs to be.

General approaches to studying need to be tailored to suit your individual personality. Don't go against this tide. Determine what kind of student you are and in which conditions you work best, and use that information to develop your study routine. Learning what kind of student you are takes time, as well as some trial and error. Frequently question the effectiveness of your study habits. Are you working as efficiently as possible? Are you accomplishing the tasks you set for yourself each week? If you are having trouble, it could be time to make a change.

Eventually, you should find yourself falling into a comfortable routine that helps you accomplish all the goals you set for yourself.

Getting Help and Helping Yourself

Making the Most of It

When you're a student, especially at a big school, it's easy to feel like a small fish in a very large sea. As you plow through miles of red tape and deal with headache-inducing bureaucracy, you can feel you have no control over your education, that your only option is to do what you are told.

Don't forget, though, that without students, there wouldn't be any education system. You are a vital part of any educational institution and, as such, you have a right to make as many demands on the system as it makes on you. Your education is at stake, and you have the right to get the best one possible — especially since you are paying for it.

If you read consumer magazines and advice guides, you'll see references to becoming an educated consumer. This means that before you make a major purchase, you do some research to get the best buy. You should similarly become an educated consumer of education. Get your money's worth from your school. Schools today are rich in resources and opportunities that can provide you with an exceptional, well-rounded education, from study-

> Be an education consumer. Take full advantage of any opportunities — academic or social — offered by your school.

abroad programs and career internships to high-tech study centers and libraries. But these opportunities are not going to come knocking on your door; you need to take active measures to find and use them. If you make the most of your education, it will eventually mean much more to you than a diploma hanging on the wall. Seek out the resources and opportunities available at your school and take advantage of them.

Help Is Out There

Throughout this book, we've been emphasizing how important it is to be an active rather than a passive student. That not only applies to your specific study tasks, but to your entire attitude as a student. You can't sit back and place your education entirely in the hands of others. Teachers, books, and other educational resources can only do so much; ultimately, you must take control of your own education if it is going to have any value.

In part, this means seeking out help when you need it. Going to school is hard work; inevitably, you are going to face some difficulties. When that happens, there is help available, but you've got to take the active role and seek it

When you need help, it's there for you. But you've got to be the one to seek it out.

out. There are many resources available to help you when you are having difficulty. If you are having trouble with coursework, you can always go talk to the professor for that class. The professor might recommend other books and additional work you might do to help you better understand the topic. Perhaps he will volunteer to offer you additional tutoring, or recommend a teaching assistant who can help you. You can also discuss any problems you are having with your advisor. Many schools also have academic advising centers where you can talk to a dean or counselor and receive academic advice of various kinds. These advisors can put you in touch with people who can help you with whatever specific academic problems you are facing.

You might find yourself grappling with emotional problems as well. School can be a very stressful place, and it can become difficult to cope. Schools do offer many forms of counseling that you can turn to. Many schools have a peer counseling center, where you can talk to a specially trained fellow student (either by phone or in person) about whatever you like. These students are trained to be nonjudgmental, and as they are your peers, they can often relate to your problems. There will also usually be a more professional kind of free counseling service available at school. If you are having any kind of trouble, you should feel free to take advantage of this. There is nothing to be ashamed of in seeking help when you need it. You won't be the only person doing this; many students find themselves grappling with various problems, which is why these services are readily available.

Finding a Mentor

Your friends and family can offer you advice on many things, but a teacher is perhaps best qualified to offer specific advice about your education. For that reason, finding a faculty member who can serve as your mentor is extremely important. In addition to offering you advice, a mentor can help you negotiate the school's bureaucracy, discuss your future career or educational plans, write letters of recommendation, and much more.

Finding a mentor will take time and effort. There's no sign-up sheet for mentors, and no professor is going to knock on your door and volunteer. You need to find a professor whom you like and respect, and then work to establish a relationship. At some point, you will take a course with a teacher you really like. You can initially see this person during office hours, and on the first couple of visits simply discuss the course. If the professor seems receptive, you can eventually ask for advice on other aspects of your education and volunteer more information about your own interests and goals. If you meet with the professor several times during the semester, you should begin to feel you are

> Try to foster a relationship with a faculty mentor and with a close peer. You can rely on these people for advice, support, and understanding.

establishing a relationship. The key to finding a professor who becomes your mentor, though, is to maintain that relationship once the semester is over. Don't let a solid relationship with a teacher slip away. Make certain you continue meeting with the teacher, even if you are no longer taking her class.

Counting on a Friend

As with a mentor, it can be tremendously helpful to have a close friend upon whom you can rely for support and understanding. And as with your mentor, it can take time to find that person and foster that kind of close relationship. But if you leave yourself open to the possibility, you will not only find yourself meeting many people, but eventually making friends. And in time, one or more of those friends will become quite close with you and you'll begin to depend on one another for support.

During the first few weeks of a semester, it is generally easy to meet people, as everyone is pretty much in the same boat. Even if you are typically shy, you should feel more comfortable during these early weeks talking to classmates and others you meet around school. Of course, many of these people will not share a bond with you. However, you only need one truly close friend; chances are that as you meet and talk to more people, you'll eventually find someone who shares many interests with you. A good strategy for meeting people is to become involved with some kind of extracurricular activity; you know from the start that these people share at least one interest with you.

Battling Stress

School can often be stressful, especially when you are juggling so many responsibilities. However, stress *is* something you can cope with and even overcome. First and foremost, stay as healthy as you can throughout the school year. Avoid junk foods, and make sure you eat regular, well-balanced meals and take vitamins. Also make an effort to get enough sleep and exercise regularly. By keeping your body in good physical condition, you will feel physically more able to grapple with work. And when things get stressful, you won't be as likely to get sick because you'll be in good condition.

When you do find yourself feeling panicked about work, there are various techniques you can use to help calm yourself down. First, following the step-by-step strategies and time management techniques outlined in this book will help alleviate stress, as you'll be approaching all of your duties in a logical, clear-headed fashion. You can also give yourself short relaxation breaks. If you feel pressured, a

> When you make a mistake, do all you can to learn from it. Understand what went wrong, ask yourself questions, and make changes.

quiet walk or listening to music with your eyes closed can revive and uplift you. You can try relaxation and meditation exercises. For example, you can close your eyes, breathe deeply, and imagine yourself at a place where you feel comfortable. The more you practice these exercises, the more quickly you'll be able to relax each time you do them. Also, by finding activities in addition to schoolwork — such as exercising or participating in extracurricular activities — that you do each week, you ensure that you'll always have a break from the grind of work.

If you're going through a particularly stressful period and these techniques don't work, then you can seek help. Talking to a friend or a peer counselor who understands the grind of student life can make you feel much better.

Learning from Mistakes

With all of the work you do as a student, inevitably you are going to make some kind of mistake. It can be a rather small one, such as screwing up an assignment or forgetting something on a test, or a large one, like failing a course. Making mistakes is part of life; it's what makes us human. Rather than becoming angry at yourself or depressed, you can try to gain something from the entire experience. Mistakes present opportunities to make changes and learn.

When you get back exams and papers, don't toss them away. Look over them carefully and read the teacher's comments. Make certain you understand exactly what you did wrong, and try to determine what you might do differently next time. If you fail a course or are generally having academic difficulty, you can take a similar approach. Try to understand exactly where the problem lies. Think about what kind of work or study habits you have, and ask yourself what kinds of changes you might make for the better. Seek help or advice from professors, advisors, or friends if necessary. Make specific changes in your routine or study habits, and see how they work. If you're still having trouble, make more changes. Eventually, you'll find yourself learning not only how to go about various study tasks, but how to grapple with problems in general. And that's a lesson that can help you long after your last day of school.

Index

A

abbreviations, shorthand techniques for, 53-55

academic advising, getting help from, 9, 147, 148-149

academic offerings, school size affecting, 5

active involvement
in listening, 36, 38, 39-40
in reading, 92-95, 119
in studying, xii-xiii, 122, 142
in thinking, 98

alarm clock
in datebook/organizer, 21
to enhance motivation, 140-141

almanac, for reference use, 19-20

anecdotes, shorthand techniques for, 53

argument, reflected in thesis statement, 103

atlas, for reference use, 19

attendance. *see also* class participation
at lectures, 35
don't leave class early, 69-70
evaluating policy for, 26
getting to class early, 41, 70
relation to class participation, 30

attitude, 33

author, identifying main concerns of, 97, 99

B

bibliography
including in essay, 106
investigating for source material, 83-84, 103

bibliography cards, creating, 103

big picture
for active reading, 93-95, 101
relation to goals, x-xii, 122
strategy for acquiring, 108

blackboard. *see also* repetition
significance of information on, 45

body language. *see* non-verbal communication

books. *see also* reading assignments; source material; textbooks
purchasing or borrowing, 15-17
required reference books, 17-18
almanac, 19-20
atlas, 19
dictionary, 18
grammar handbook, 19
style manual, 19
thesaurus, 18

bookstore
investigating required reading in, 10
purchasing books in, 15-16, 17
purchasing supplies in, 25

breaks
during studying, 108, 139, 141
for relaxation, 150-151

C

calendar, for staying organized, 20-21, 24, 125

campus visits, to research schools, 4, 6, 7

charts and diagrams, shorthand techniques for, 57-58

citations, for source material, 106

classes. *see also* attendance; courses; lectures
first week evaluation of, 25-26
student responsibilities in, 27-28, 81
study schedule for, 126-135

class participation. *see also* attendance
affect on grades, 29, 30, 31-32
evaluating requirements for, 26
posture recommendations for, 37
student responsibilities for, 27-28, 81

college guides, for researching schools, 2-3

comfort, pros and cons of, 76, 141, 142, 143

comments, recommended format for, 32

communication skills. *see also* listening skills; non-verbal communication
affecting note taking, 34-35, 38
importance of, xiv-xv, 122

computers
laptop use in class, 43-44
recommendations for, 21-23, 24